HARCOURT SCIENCE

TEACHING RESOURCES

Harcourt School Publishers

Orlando • Boston • Dallas • Chicago • San Diego

www.harcourtschool.com

HARCOURT SCIENCE
Contents

Harcourt

Harcourt

School-Home Connection

Chapter Content

In science we are beginning a chapter that focuses on plants. Plants have specific needs that must be met in order for them to thrive and grow. These needs are covered in the chapter, along with a thorough exploration of the parts of plants, how plants make food, and the purpose and function of seeds.

Science Process Skills

Learning to **observe** carefully is one of the most important skills of science. Invite your child to take a walk in your neighborhood to look at plants. Ask your child to explain the process a seed goes through as it grows into a mature plant. Let your child point out and name the different parts of the plants you see. Record these observations in a notebook. Later in the year, take another walk, and record any differences you observe in the same plants.

Science Fun

Children's books about science can serve a double purpose. While entertaining young readers, they can also help clarify scientific concepts. This helps students reinforce what they are learning in the classroom.

From Seed to Plant by Gail Gibbons (Holiday House, 1993).

From Seed to Plant represents the transformation of seeds into full plants in clear and simple language. The book explores the intricate relationship between seeds and the plants that they produce. The colorful illustrations serve to expand the reader's understanding of the basic science of plants.

Activity Materials from Home

Dear Family Member:

In order to do the activities in this chapter, we will need some materials that you may have around your home. Please note the items to the right. If possible, please send these things to school with your child.

Your help and support are appreciated!

____ **brown paper bag**
____ **3 kinds of seeds**
____ **empty 0.5-L**
     plastic bottle
____ **twist ties**

Harcourt

La escuela y la casa

Harcourt Ciencias

Contenido del capítulo

Hoy comenzamos un capítulo de ciencias sobre las plantas. Las plantas tienen necesidades específicas que deben satisfacer para poder crecer y prosperar. Estas necesidades se presentan en el capítulo, a través de una exploración detallada de las partes de las plantas, cómo las plantas producen alimentos y el propósito y función de las semillas.

Destrezas del proceso científico

Aprender a **observar** detalladamente es una de las destrezas más importantes de las ciencias. Invite a su hijo(a) a caminar por su vecindario para observar las plantas. Pida a su hijo(a) que explique el proceso por el que pasa una semilla a medida que crece hasta que se convierte en una planta madura. Permita que su hijo(a) señale y nombre las diferentes partes de una planta que ve. Anote estas observaciones en un cuaderno. Más tarde durante el año, caminen por el vecindario nuevamente y anoten cualquier diferencia que puedan observar en las mismas plantas.

Diversión

Los libros infantiles sobre las ciencias pueden tener dos propósitos. Además de entretener a los lectores jóvenes, también pueden ayudar a clarificar conceptos científicos. Esto ayuda a los estudiantes a reforzar lo que aprenden en el salón de clases.

From Seed to Plant de Gail Gibbons (Holiday House, 1993).

From Seed to Plant de Gail Gibbons representa la transformación de las semillas en plantas en un lenguaje claro y sencillo. El libro explora la relación compleja entre las semillas y las plantas que producen. Las ilustraciones a color sirven para ampliar la comprensión de las ciencias básicas de las plantas.

Materiales de casa para la actividad

Querido familiar:

Para hacer las actividades en este capítulo, necesitaremos algunos materiales que tal vez tenga en la casa. Observe los artículos de la lista de la derecha. Si es posible, por favor envíe estas cosas con su hijo(a) a la escuela.

¡Gracias por su ayuda y su apoyo!

____ bolsa de papel de color café
____ 3 tipos de semillas
____ botella plástica vacía de 0.5L
____ alambritos

Harcourt

School-Home Connection

Chapter Content

We are beginning a chapter on a number of important aspects of animals. Different kinds of animals have different needs, but all share the need for food, water, air, and shelter. Your child will learn about animal species and what threatens them. How species become extinct is also discussed.

Science Process Skills

Most people make daily observations of the world around them. Real understanding, however, comes from thinking about observations and making **inferences** about what is observed. This game will help your child gather data and make a logical inference using that data, while reinforcing your child's understanding of the different types of animals.

Animal 20-Questions

Play a question game about animals with your child. Together, write some questions, such as Are you a mammal, a bird, or a reptile? Do you have fur or feathers? What kind of place do you live in? What do you eat? You can find more qualities of animals in your child's science book. One player chooses an animal to think of. The other asks the questions until the animal is identified.

Science Fun

Children's books about animals can be entertaining as well as instructive. Accurate illustrations serve as an added learning feature. Children can add to the information they have gathered in the classroom by reading a book that complements a lesson.

Animal Senses: How Animals, See, Hear, Taste, Smell and Feel by Pamela Hickman (Kids Can Publishers, 1998).

Pamela Hickman has written a book on animal senses. *Animal Senses: How Animals, See, Hear, Taste, Smell and Feel* presents intriguing text and science activities. Readers will find plenty of information about how different animals not only see, hear, smell, taste, and feel what's around them, but also how they pick up on other clues about their surroundings by sensing heat, electricity, and magnetic fields.

Read this book together with your child. Work together to make a list of all the ways animals gather information about the world around them.

Activity Materials from Home

Dear Family Member:

In order to do the activities in this chapter, we will need some materials that you may have around your home. Please note the items to the right. If possible, please send these things to school with your child.

Your help and support are appreciated!

____ **metal cans**
____ **cotton batting**
____ **rocks**
____ **gravel**
____ **dried fish food**

La escuela y la casa

Contenido del capítulo

Hoy comenzamos un nuevo capítulo de ciencias sobre un número de aspectos importantes de los animales. Diferentes tipos de animales tienen diferentes necesidades, pero todos comparten las necesidades de alimento, agua, aire y refugio. Su hijo(a) aprenderá sobre las especies de los animales y lo que las pone en peligro. También aprenderán cómo las especies se hacen extintas.

Destrezas del proceso científico

La mayoría de las personas hacen observaciones diariamente del mundo que los rodea. Sin embargo, la comprensión proviene del pensar sobre las observaciones y del hacer **inferencias** sobre lo que se observa. Este juego ayudará a su hijo(a) a recopilar datos, mientras refuerza la comprensión de su hijo(a) sobre los diferentes tipos de animales.

20 Preguntas sobre animales

Juegue un juego de preguntas sobre los animales con su hijo(a). Escriban algunas preguntas como: ¿Eres un mamífero, un ave o un reptil? ¿Tienes pelaje o plumas? ¿En qué clase de lugar vives? ¿Qué comes? Usted puede encontrar más cualidades de los animales en el libro de ciencias de su hijo(a). Un jugador piensa en un animal y el otro jugador hace preguntas hasta que identifica el animal.

Harcourt Ciencias

Diversión

Los libros infantiles sobre animales pueden ser tanto divertidos como instructivos. Las ilustraciones precisas sirven como una característica adicional de aprendizaje. Los niños pueden leer un libro que complemente una lección para agregar información que han recopilado en el salón de clases.

Animal Senses: How Animals, See, Hear, Taste, Smell and Feel de Pamela Hickman (Kids Can Publishers, 1998).

Pamela Hickman has written a book on animal senses. *Animal Senses: How Animals, See, Hear, Taste, Smell and Feel* presenta un texto fascinante y actividades científicas. Los lectores encontrarán información completa no solamente sobre cómo animales diferentes ven, oyen, huelen, saborean y sienten lo que está a su alrededor sino también cómo recopilan pistas sobre su alrededor al percibir calor, electricidad y campos magnéticos.

Lea este libro con su hijo(a). Trabaje con su hijo(a) para hacer una lista de todas las formas en que los animales recopilan información sobre el mundo que los rodea.

Materiales de casa para la actividad

Querido familiar:

Para hacer las actividades en este capítulo, necesitaremos algunos materiales que tal vez tenga en la casa. Observe los artículos de la lista de la derecha. Si es posible, por favor envíe estas cosas con su hijo(a) a la escuela.

¡Gracias por su ayuda y su apoyo!

____ **latas de metal**
____ **algodón en rama**
____ **rocas**
____ **gravilla**
____ **alimento seco para peces**

School-Home Connection

Chapter Content

Today we begin a new chapter in science. We will be learning about ecosystems—the places on Earth where living things are found. We will be studying different types of forest ecosystems, water ecosystems, and desert ecosystems. We will also be doing several activities, including observing environments to see what living and nonliving things can be found in each and making a model of a desert ecosystem.

Science Process Skills

Learning to **observe** carefully is an important skill in science. This activity will help your child develop his or her ability to observe.

Gather a number of different household objects, such as a comb, a brush, a book, a dish—things that you have around the house. Show them as a group to your child for about 15 seconds. Then cover the objects. See how many items your child can remember. Change the objects several times, and see if your child improves.

Science Fun

Whether you live in a rural, suburban, or urban area, you live in an environment that includes living and nonliving things.

What to Do

Pick out a small area and plan an observation walk. You might choose a nearby park, field, or forest, or you may just walk around your yard. Before you go on the walk, talk about the things you will be looking for, such as living things, nonliving things, and sources of food and water. Make a chart like this one that you can fill in as you walk.

Our Local Environment		
Living Things	Nonliving Things	Other Observations

As you take your walk, record your observations. Use your observations to write a short story describing something in your local environment.

Activity Materials from Home

Dear Family Member:

To do the activities in this chapter, we will need some materials that you may have at home. Please note the items at the right. If possible, please send these things to school with your child.

Your help and support are appreciated!

____ **wire clothes hanger**
____ **dried beans**
____ **plastic wrap**
____ **shoe box**
____ **small rocks**
____ **gravel**
____ **sand**

La escuela y la casa

Harcourt Ciencias

Contenido del capítulo

Hoy comenzamos un nuevo capítulo de ciencias. Aprenderemos sobre los ecosistemas, los lugares de la Tierra donde se encuentran los seres vivos. Estudiaremos diferentes tipos de ecosistemas forestales, acuáticos y desérticos. También haremos varias actividades, que incluyen observar los medio ambientes para determinar qué seres vivos y no vivos se pueden hallar en cada uno y hacer un modelo de un ecosistema desértico.

Destrezas del proceso científico

Aprender a **observar** detalladamente es una destreza importante de las ciencias. Esta actividad ayudará a su hijo(a) a desarrollar su habilidad de observar.

Recopile diferentes objetos caseros como un peine, un cepillo, un libro, un plato, cosas que tiene en la casa. Muéstrelas a su hijo(a), en un grupo durante 15 segundos. Luego tape los objetos. Vea cuántos objetos puede recordar su hijo(a). Cambie los objetos varias veces y vea si su hijo(a) mejora.

Diversión

No importa si viven en una área rural, un suburbio o una área urbana, viven en un medio ambiente que incluye seres vivos y no vivos.

Lo que vas a hacer

Elige un área pequeña y planea una caminata de observación. Podrías elegir un parque, un campo o un bosque cercano o podrías caminar por tu patio. Antes de ir a caminar, habla sobre las cosas que buscarás como seres vivos, no vivos y fuentes de alimento y agua. Haz una tabla como ésta que puedas llenar mientras caminas.

Nuestro medio ambiente local		
Seres vivos	Seres no vivos	Otras observaciones

Mientras caminas, anota tus observaciones. Usa tus observaciones para escribir un cuento corto que describa algo en tu medio ambiente local.

Materiales de casa para la actividad

Querido familiar:

Para hacer las actividades en este capítulo, necesitaremos algunos materiales que tal vez tenga en la casa. Observe los artículos de la lista de la derecha. Si es posible, por favor envíe estas cosas con su hijo(a) a la escuela.

¡Gracias por su ayuda y su apoyo!

____ **gancho de alambre de ropa**
____ **frijoles secos**
____ **papel de plástico**
____ **caja de zapatos**
____ **rocas pequeñas**
____ **gravilla**
____ **arena**

School-Home Connection

Chapter Content

Today we begin a new chapter in science. We will be learning about the ways that living things depend on one another. Your child will learn how living things get food, and how all animals are in some way dependent on plants for food. This idea will be reinforced in activities in which students make model food chains and food webs, tracing the flow of energy from plants to animals.

Science Process Skills

Who Eats What?: Food Chains and Food Webs by Patricia Lauber and Holly Keller (Harpercrest, 1995).

Making accurate **observations** is an important science skill. Often, we directly observe the world around us. But sometimes, it is difficult to see all the steps in a process in nature. Use the book *Who Eats What?* to help your child make observations about how food energy moves from one living thing to another. After browsing through the book, have your child choose several food chains and trace with a finger the movement of energy from plants to animals to other animals.

ScienceFun

A food chain is a model of how energy moves in the real world. You can use what your child observed in *Who Eats What?* to make personal food chains that include your family's favorite foods.

What You Need

- index cards
- yarn
- tape
- science book or other reference book

What to Do

1. Have your child draw pictures on index cards showing the chains for the things they eat, such as milk, which came from a cow, which ate grass. Connect the cards using yarn and tape.

2. Ask each family member to make a different food chain. After your child finishes Lesson 3, have him or her combine the chains to make a food web.

Activity Materials from Home

Dear Family Member:

To do the activities in this chapter, we will need some materials that you may have around your home. Please note the items listed at the right. If possible, please send these things to school with your child.

Your help and support are appreciated!

____ **blank index cards**
____ **yarn or string**
____ **tape or glue**
____ **poster board**

Harcourt

La escuela y la casa

Contenido del capítulo

Hoy comenzamos un nuevo capítulo de ciencias. Aprenderemos sobre las maneras en que los seres vivos dependen unos de otros. Su hijo(a) aprenderá cómo obtienen su alimento los seres vivos y cómo todos los animales dependen de una forma u otra de las plantas para alimentarse. Esta idea se reforzará en actividades en las que los estudiantes harán modelos de cadenas alimenticias y ciclos alimenticios, trazando el flujo de energía de las plantas a los animales.

Destrezas del proceso científico

Who Eats What?: Food Chains and Food Webs de Patricia Lauber and Holly Keller (Harpercrest, 1995).

Hacer **observaciones** precisas es una destreza importante de las ciencias. A menudo, observamos directamente el mundo que nos rodea. Pero a veces, es difícil ver todos los pasos en un proceso de la naturaleza. Use el libro *Who Eats What?* para ayudar a su hijo(a) a hacer observaciones sobre cómo se mueve la energía alimenticia de un ser vivo a otro. Después de hojear el libro, pida a su hijo(a) que elija varias cadenas alimenticias y trace con un dedo el movimiento de la energía desde las plantas hasta los animales y hasta otros animales.

Diversión

Una cadena alimenticia es un modelo de cómo la energía se moviliza en el mundo real. Usted puede usar lo que su hijo(a) observó en *Who Eats What?* para hacer cadenas alimenticias propias que incluyan los alimentos favoritos de su familia.

Lo que necesitas

- tarjetas
- estambre
- cinta adhesiva
- libro de ciencias u otro libro de referencia

Lo que vas a hacer

1. Pida a su hijo(a) que haga ilustraciones en las tarjetas que muestren las cadenas para las cosas que comen como leche, la cual proviene de la vaca, que comió hierba. Una las tarjetas usando estambre y cinta adhesiva.

2. Pida a cada miembro de la familia que haga una cadena alimenticia diferente. Después de que su hijo(a) termine la Lección 3, pídale que combine las cadenas para hacer un ciclo alimenticio.

Materiales de casa para la actividad

Querido familiar:

Para hacer las actividades en este capítulo, necesitaremos algunos materiales que tal vez tenga en la casa. Observe los artículos de la lista de la derecha. Si es posible, por favor envíe estas cosas con su hijo(a) a la escuela.

¡Gracias por su ayuda y su apoyo!

____ **tarjetas en blanco**
____ **estambre o hilo**
____ **cinta adhesiva o pegamento**
____ **cartón**

Harcourt

School-Home Connection

Chapter Content

We are beginning a new chapter in science. We will be learning about the composition of the Earth, how rocks form, and fossils. We will explore the properties of minerals, classify rocks by the way they formed and determine one way the relative age of a fossil can be determined.

Science Process Skills

Comparing involves looking at two or more things and saying what is the same and what is different about them. In this chapter, students will compare igneous, sedimentary, and metamorphic rocks and discuss their differences and their similarities.

Encourage your child to start a collection of rocks gathered from your neighborhood or from areas to which you travel together. Help your child keep a rock collecting notebook, noting where and when different rocks are found. Have them compare the rocks in the collection and say how they are the same and different.

Science Fun

Children's books about rock collecting can be entertaining as well as instructive. Read the book together, then pick one or two of the activities below to try.

Let's Go Rock Collecting by Roma Gans and Holly Keller (Harpercrest, 1997).

- Pick one type of rock, and look for information about its formation, hardness, and uses.

- Have your child compare the cross-section of Earth to the information presented in his or her science book.

- Use your finger to trace the rise and eruption of lava in the cross-section of a volcano.

- Look for two children exploring a Roman road, finding fossils, mixing cement, and collecting rocks. Write a story about one of their adventures.

Activity Materials from Home

Dear Family Member:

In order to do the activities in this chapter, we will need some materials that you may have around your home. Please note the items to the right. If possible, please send these things to school with your child.

Your help and support are appreciated!

____ **modeling clay of different colors**
____ **seashells**
____ **wax paper**

Harcourt

La escuela y la casa

Harcourt Ciencias

Contenido del capítulo

Hoy comenzamos un nuevo capítulo de ciencias.
Aprenderemos sobre la composición de la Tierra,
cómo se forman las rocas y los fósiles.
Exploraremos las propiedades de los minerales,
clasificaremos rocas de acuerdo a la manera en que
se formaron y hallaremos una manera de
determinar la edad relativa de un fósil.

Destrezas del proceso científico

Comparar implica observar dos o más cosas y decir
que en qué se parecen y en qué se diferencian. En
este capítulo, los estudiantes compararán rocas
ígneas, sedimentarias y metamórficas y comentarán
sus diferencias y semejanzas.

Anime a su hijo(a) a que comience una colección de
rocas que recoge en su vecindario o en áreas a las
que hayan visitado. Ayude a su hijo(a) a que tenga
un cuaderno de colección de rocas para que anote
cuándo y dónde se hallaron las rocas. Pídale que
compare las rocas de la colección y diga en qué se
parecen y en qué se diferencian.

Diversión

Los libros infantiles sobre las colecciones de rocas
pueden ser tanto divertidos como instructivos. Lean
el libro y luego elijan una o dos de las actividades de
abajo para probar.

> *Let's Go Rock Collecting* de Roma Gans y
> Holly Keller (Harpercrest, 1997).
>
> - Elige un tipo de roca y busca información
>   sobre su formación, dureza y usos.
>
> - Pida a su hijo(a) que compare el corte
>   transversal de la Tierra con la información
>   que se presenta en su libro de ciencias.
>
> - Usa tu dedo para trazar el ascenso y la
>   erupción de la lava en el corte transversal
>   de un volcán.
>
> - Busca dos niños que exploran un camino
>   romano, buscan fósiles, mezclan cemento y
>   recogen rocas. Escribe un cuento sobre una
>   de sus aventuras.

Materiales de casa para la actividad

Querido familiar:

Para hacer las actividades en este capítulo, necesitaremos
algunos materiales que tal vez tenga en la casa. Observe
los artículos de la lista de la derecha. Si es posible, por
favor envíe estas cosas con su hijo(a) a la escuela.

¡Gracias por su ayuda y su apoyo!

____ **plastilina de diferentes colores**
____ **conchas de mar**
____ **papel encerado**

School-Home Connection

Harcourt Science

Chapter Content

Our science class is beginning a chapter on Earth's landforms. Landforms are the shapes or features found on Earth's surface. They include mountains, valleys, canyons, plains, plateaus, and barrier islands. Weathering and erosion change landforms slowly. Volcanoes and earthquakes change landforms rapidly.

Science Process Skills

Drawing conclusions is an important science skill. To draw a conclusion, a scientist makes observations, collects data, and makes inferences about what the data mean. The scientist also thinks about what he or she already knows. When all of this information is considered, a conclusion about how something happened is drawn.

You can help your child practice drawing conclusions. Use several colors of clay or dough. Put the clay in layers, and then bend or fold the layers to make different shapes. Have your child observe the shapes, and then tell you what you did to make the shape. Have your child list the clues that led him or her to draw the conclusion about how the shape was made.

Science Fun

Children's books about landforms can be entertaining as well as instructive. The following book will reinforce what your child is learning in the chapter, as well as provide a fun reading experience.

How Mountains Are Made by Kathleen Weidner Zoehfield and James Graham Hale (HarperTrophy, 1995).

In this book four children and a dog climb a mountain trail. Along the way, the characters explain Earth's structure. They discuss the different types of mountains and how they were formed.

After reading this book together, ask your child to choose one type of mountain and make a drawing detailing its formation. If you have clay available from the **Science Process Skills** activity, have your child make a model of the type of mountain he or she chose to draw.

Activity Materials from Home

Dear Family Member:

In order to do the activities in this chapter, we will need some materials that you may have around the house. Please note the items to the right. If possible, please send these things to school with your child.

Your help and support are appreciated!

____ sand
____ glass jar with lid
____ wax paper
____ baking soda
____ red, green, and blue food coloring
____ white vinegar

Harcourt

La escuela y la casa

Harcourt Ciencias

Contenido del capítulo

Hoy comenzamos un nuevo capítulo de ciencias sobre los accidentes geográficos. Los accidentes geográficos son las formas o características que se hallan en la superficie de la Tierra. Incluyen las montañas, los valles, los cañones, las llanuras, las mesetas y las islas de coral. La degradación y la erosión cambian los accidentes geográficos lentamente. Los volcanes y los terremotos cambian los accidentes geográficos rápidamente.

Destrezas del proceso científico

Sacar conclusiones es una destreza importante de las ciencias. Para sacar una conclusión, un científico hace observaciones, recopila datos y hace inferencias sobre lo que significa cada dato. El científico también piensa sobre lo que ya sabe. Cuando se considera toda esta información, se saca una conclusión sobre algo que ha sucedido.

Usted puede ayudar a su hijo(a) a que practique a sacar conclusiones. Use varios colores de plastilina o masa. Ponga la plastilina en capas y luego doble las capas para hacer diferentes figuras. Pida a su hijo(a) que observe las figuras y que luego le diga qué hizo usted para hacer esa figura. Pida a su hijo(a) que haga una lista de pistas que le permita sacar conclusiones sobre cómo se hizo la figura.

Diversión

Los libros infantiles sobre los accidentes geográficos pueden ser tanto divertidos como instructivos. El siguiente libro reforzará lo que su hijo(a) aprende en el capítulo, así como también proporciona una experiencia de lectura divertida.

How Mountains Are Made de Kathleen Weidner Zoehfield y James Graham Hale (Harper Trophy, 1995).

En este libro, cuatro niños y un perro escalan el sendero de una montaña. A lo largo del camino, los personajes explican la estructura de la Tierra. Comentan los diferentes tipos de montañas y cómo se formaron.

Después de leer este libro con su hijo(a), pídale que elija un tipo de montaña y que haga un dibujo detallado de su formación. Si tiene plastilina disponible de la actividad de **Destrezas del proceso científico,** pida a su hijo(a) que haga un modelo del tipo de montaña que ha elegido dibujar.

Materiales de casa para la actividad

Querido familiar:

Para hacer las actividades en este capítulo, necesitaremos algunos materiales que tal vez tenga en la casa. Observe los artículos de la lista de la derecha. Si es posible, por favor envíe estas cosas con su hijo(a) a la escuela.

¡Gracias por su ayuda y su apoyo!

_____ arena
_____ frasco de vidrio con tapa
_____ papel encerado
_____ bicarbonato
_____ colorante rojo, verde y azul
_____ vinagre blanco

Harcourt

School-Home Connection

Harcourt Science

Chapter Content

Our science class is beginning a chapter on soils. We will be learning that it takes a long time for new soil to form and why it is so important to conserve soil. We will be doing activities that focus on the parts that make up soil, the different types of soil, and ways plants help keep soil from washing away.

Science Process Skills

Predicting involves analyzing what you know and, based on that information, saying what you think will happen in the future. This activity can give your child practice in predicting outcomes.

Have your child predict whether each event listed below will help or hurt the soil. Have your child tell you why he or she made each prediction.

- A worm burrows in the soil. It leaves its wastes in the soil.

- A heavy rain washes soil from a farmer's field.

- A plant breaks a rock into small pieces.

- A gardener plants grass in a muddy area in her yard.

Science Fun

In Lesson 3, your child will be learning about different ways of slowing soil erosion. In this activity, you can build some model fields and test some soil conservation methods.

What You Need

- large rectangular baking pan
- watering can
- potting soil
- grass seed or sod

What to Do

1. Make a landscape out of soil in the pan. Include several hills and valleys.

2. Cover some of the hills with sod (or sprout grass seed on some of the hills). Leave some others bare.

3. Sprinkle water over your landscape, and observe how the grass affects the erosion of soil.

4. Expand your experiment. Make some terraces on your hills, or use different types of soil or different plants. Keep a record of how each change affected the rate of soil erosion.

Activity Materials from Home

Dear Family Member:

In order to do the activities in this chapter, we will need some materials that you may have around the house. Please note the items to the right. If possible, please send these things to school with your child.

Your help and support are appreciated!

____ **dry, unsweetened cereal**
____ **plastic wrap**
____ **paper plates**
____ **baking pans**
____ **large foam cups**

La escuela y la casa

Harcourt Ciencias

Contenido del capítulo

Hoy comenzamos un nuevo capítulo de ciencias sobre los suelos. Aprenderemos que toma mucho tiempo para que se forme un suelo nuevo y por qué es tan importante conservar el suelo. Haremos actividades que enfocan las partes que forman el suelo, los diferentes tipos de suelo y las formas en que las plantas ayudan a proteger el suelo de ser arrasado.

Destrezas del proceso científico

Predecir implica analizar lo que sabes y basado en esa información, decir lo que crees que pasará en el futuro. Esta actividad le puede dar a su hijo(a) la práctica de predecir los resultados.

Pida a su hijo(a) que prediga si cada suceso en la lista de abajo ayudará o dañará el suelo. Pida a su hijo(a) que le diga por qué hizo esa predicción.

• La madriguera de un gusano en el suelo. Éste deja sus desperdicios en el suelo.

• Una lluvia fuerte arrastra el suelo de los campos de un agricultor.

• Una planta rompe una roca en pequeños fragmentos.

• Un jardinero siembra grama en un área fangosa de su jardín.

Diversión

En la Lección 3, su hijo(a) aprenderá sobre las diferentes formas de disminuir la erosión del suelo. En esta actividad, puedes hacer algunos modelos de campos y probar algunos métodos de conservación del suelo.

Lo que necesitas

• bandeja grande rectangular
• regadera de plantas y flores
• semillas de grama o césped
• tierra para plantar

Lo que vas a hacer

1. Elabora un paisaje hecho de la tierra en la bandeja. Incluye muchas colinas y valles.

2. Con su hijo(a), cubra algunas colinas con césped (o coloque semillas de grama en algunas colinas). Deje algunas descubiertas.

3. Rieguen con agua el paisaje y observen cómo la grama afecta la erosión del suelo.

4. Extiendan su experimento. Coloquen algunas terrazas en sus colinas o usen diferentes tipos de tierra o diferentes plantas. Anoten cómo cada cambio afectó el porcentaje de la erosión del suelo.

Materiales de casa para la actividad

Querido familiar:

Para hacer las actividades de este capítulo, necesitaremos algunos materiales que tal vez tenga en la casa. Observe los artículos de la lista de la derecha. Si es posible, por favor envíe estas cosas con su hijo(a) a la escuela.

¡Gracias por su ayuda y su apoyo!

____ cereal seco y sin dulce
____ papel de plástico
____ platos de papel
____ bandejas
____ vasitos grandes de estireno

Harcourt

School-Home Connection

Harcourt Science

Chapter Content

Our science class is beginning a chapter on Earth's resources and ways to conserve those resources. We will learn that Earth holds many resources, some of which are renewable, and some of which are not. There are a number of ways to retrieve resources, including mining for gold and pumping oil.

Science Process Skills

Using numbers helps a person tell others exactly what data has been collected. You can give your child practice in using numbers by doing a pantry survey. Look through your kitchen cupboards and count the items made of aluminum (juice and soft-drink cans), steel (most canned items), and plastic. Work together to make a bar graph showing how many items of each kind you found. Discuss the resources needed to make these materials. Are any of them renewable? (Containers made from paper are made of renewable resources.)

ScienceFun

Children's books about conserving resources can be entertaining as well as instructive. You can find this book, or a similar book, at your local library.

Earth-Friendly Outdoor Fun: How to Make Fabulous Games, Gardens, and Other Projects from Reusable Objects by George Pfiffner (John Wiley & Sons, 1996).

Together with your child, browse through the 25 fun-to-do projects this book contains. The book includes step-by-step instructions on how to convert materials such as scrap cardboard and plastic bottles into items for outdoor fun and use. Projects include making games such as bowling and pick-up sticks, carrying out gardening activities, making a kite, making a giant bubble maker, and making a boomerang. Pick one of the projects to do.

Activity Materials from Home

Dear Family Member:

In order to do the activities in this chapter, we will need some materials that you may have around the house. Please note the items to the right. If possible, please send these things to school with your child.

Your help and support are appreciated!

____ oatmeal-raisin cookies
____ paper plates
____ used, washed aluminum cans
____ large plastic trash bags

Harcourt

La escuela y la casa

Harcourt Ciencias

Contenido del capítulo

Hoy comenzamos un nuevo capítulo de ciencias sobre los recursos de la Tierra y la forma de conservar estos recursos. Aprenderemos que la Tierra tiene muchos recursos, algunos de los cuales son renovables y algunos de ellos no. Hay un número de maneras de salvar los recursos, incluidos la minería de oro y la extracción de petróleo.

Destrezas del proceso científico

Usar los números ayuda a las personas a decirle a otras exactamente los datos que se han recopilado. Usted puede hacer que su hijo(a) practique el uso de números al realizar una encuesta sobre la despensa. Busque en los armarios de su cocina y cuente los artículos hechos de aluminio (latas de jugos y de refrescos), de acero (la mayoría de los artículos enlatados) y de plástico. Trabaje con su hijo(a) para hacer una gráfica de barras y mostrar cuántos artículos de cada tipo encontró. Comente los recursos necesarios para hacer estos materiales. ¿Son renovables algunos de ellos? (Los recipientes hechos de papel son hechos de recursos renovables.)

Diversión

Los libros infantiles sobre la conservación de los recursos pueden ser tanto divertidos como instructivos. Usted puede encontrar este libro o un libro similar en su biblioteca local.

Earth-Friendly Outdoor Fun: How to Make Fabulous Games, Gardens, and Other Projects from Reusable Objects de George Pfiffner (John Wiley & Sons, 1996).

Junto con su hijo(a), hojee los 25 proyectos de cosas divertidas que contiene este libro. El libro incluye instrucciones paso por paso sobre cómo convertir materiales, como un pedazo de cartulina y botellas de plástico, en artículos de uso y diversión al aire libre. Los proyectos incluyen hacer juegos como el boliche y recoger palitos, llevar a cabo actividades de jardinería, hacer una cometa, hacer un soplador de burbujas gigante y hacer un bumerang. Elija uno de los proyectos y háganlo.

Materiales de casa para la actividad

Querido familiar:

Para hacer las actividades de este capítulo, necesitaremos algunos materiales que tal vez tenga en la casa. Observe los artículos de la lista de la derecha. Si es posible, por favor envíe estas cosas con su hijo(a) a la escuela.

¡Gracias por su ayuda y su apoyo!

_____ galletas de avena y pasas
_____ platos de papel
_____ latas de aluminio usadas y lavadas
_____ bolsas de plástico de basura grandes

Harcourt

School-Home Connection

Harcourt Science

Chapter Content

Today in science we begin a chapter about water. In this chapter your child will learn how much water covers Earth's surface, where most of Earth's water is found, and what the water cycle is.

Science Process Skills

Using numbers can help people accurately communicate the data they have collected. This activity will give your child practice in using numbers.

Find out how much water is lost by a dripping faucet. Set a faucet to drip. Place a large measuring cup underneath the faucet. Check the amount of water collected in 1, 5, and 10 minutes.

Repeat the activity, changing how fast the faucet drips. Help your child compare the data you collected by asking questions such as these.

- When did we collect the most water? (when the faucet dripped fastest)

- When did we collect the least water? (when the faucet dripped slowest)

- Why should water leaks and drips be stopped?

Science Fun

The movement of water from Earth's surface to the air and back is called the water cycle. Plants play an important part in this cycle. Plants absorb water from the ground and release it to the air through their leaves.

What You Need

- houseplant
- small plastic bag
- twist-tie or tape
- water

What to Do

1. Put a plastic bag around one leafy branch of the plant.

2. Tightly secure the bag with a twist-tie or tape.

3. Write down what the plant and bag look like. Draw pictures if you wish.

4. Water the plant, then place it in a well-lit spot.

5. After an hour again observe the plant. Compare what the bag looked like before and after this investigation. Have your child identify what is now on the inside of the bag (water).

Activity Materials from Home

Dear Family Member:

To do the activities in this chapter, we will need some materials that you may have at home. Please note the items at the right. If possible, please send these things to school with your child.

Your help and support are appreciated!

____ masking tape
____ four identical jars
____ salt
____ 2 jar lids

Harcourt

La escuela y la casa

Contenido del capítulo

Hoy comenzamos un nuevo capítulo de ciencias sobre el agua. En este capítulo su hijo(a) aprenderá cuánta agua cubre la superficie de la Tierra, dónde se halla la mayor cantidad de agua y cuál es el ciclo del agua.

Destrezas del proceso científico

Usar números puede ayudar a las personas a comunicar con precisión los datos que han recopilado. Esta actividad le dará a su hijo(a) la práctica de usar números.

Determine qué cantidad de agua se pierde al gotear un grifo. Abra un grifo para que gotee. Coloque una taza de medir debajo del grifo. Revise la cantidad de agua recopilada en 1, 5 y 10 minutos.

Repita la actividad cambiando la velocidad de las gotas del grifo. Ayude a su hijo(a) a comparar los datos que usted recopiló haciendo preguntas como éstas:

• ¿Cuándo recolectamos mayor cantidad de agua? (cuando el grifo goteó más rápido)

• ¿Cuándo recolectamos menor cantidad de agua? (cuando el grifo goteó más lento)

• ¿Por qué se deben detener las goteras y los escapes?

Diversión

El movimiento del agua desde la superficie de la Tierra hasta el aire y viceversa, se conoce como el ciclo del agua. Las plantas juegan un papel importante en este ciclo. Las plantas absorben el agua de la tierra y la liberan al aire a través de sus hojas.

Lo que necesitas

• plantas caseras
• alambrito o cinta adhesiva
• bolsa de plástico pequeña
• agua

Lo que vas a hacer

1. Coloque con su hijo(a) la bolsa de plástico alrededor de una rama frondosa de la planta.

2. Aseguren la bolsa atándola con un alambrito o cinta adhesiva.

3. Escriba con su hijo(a) cómo se ve la planta y la bolsa. Pueden dibujar si lo desean.

4. Rieguen la planta, luego colóquenla en un lugar con bastante luz.

5. Después de una hora observen la planta nuevamente. Comparen cómo se ve la bolsa antes y después de esta investigación. Pídale a su hijo(a) que identifique lo que hay ahora dentro de la bolsa (agua).

Materiales de casa para la actividad

Querido familiar:

Para hacer las actividades en este capítulo, necesitaremos algunos materiales que tal vez tenga en la casa. Observe los artículos de la lista de la derecha. Si es posible, por favor envíe estas cosas con su hijo(a) a la escuela.

¡Gracias por su ayuda y su apoyo!

____ **cinta adhesiva de papel**
____ **cuatro frascos idénticos**
____ **sal**
____ **2 tapas de frasco**

School-Home Connection

Harcourt Science

Chapter Content

Our science class is beginning a chapter on observing weather. We will investigate the layers of the atmosphere, and discover that weather happens mostly in the atmosphere's lowest layer. We will be making our own thermometer to help us measure the temperature of the air. We will also investigate how weather measurements are combined on a weather map.

Science Process Skills

When scientists **compare,** they determine how two things are the same and different. You can use the daily newspaper to help your child compare weather conditions in different areas of the country.

Each day for a week, examine the weather page in your local paper. Note what the weather will be in your area and in your state. Pick a state or city to the west of you, and each day compare your weather to the weather in that location. Keep track of the weather in both locations. At the end of the week, see if you can find any trends. (Weather often moves from west to east in the United States.)

Science Fun

The weight of air presses down on everything on Earth's surface. This activity demonstrates an everyday use of air pressure.

What You Need

- clear plastic straw
- clean plastic jar with lid
- awl
- clay
- water

What to Do

1. Fill the jar with water. Use the straw to suck some of the water out of the jar.

2. CAUTION: Have an adult use an awl to poke a hole through the jar's lid. The hole should be just big enough for the straw to fit through.

3. Put the straw through the hole. Seal any gaps around the straw with clay.

4. Try to suck water up the straw.

Explanation: Air pressure forces water up a straw. When the jar is sealed, air can't press on the water. The straw doesn't work.

Activity Materials from Home

Dear Family Member:

To do the activities in this chapter, we will need some materials that you may have around your home. Please note the items listed at the right. If possible, please send these things to school with your child.

Your help and support are appreciated!

____ **paper towels**
____ **plastic cups**
____ **index cards**
____ **clear drinking straws**
____ **clay**

Harcourt

La escuela y la casa

Harcourt Ciencias

Contenido del capítulo

Hoy comenzamos un nuevo capítulo de ciencias sobre el clima. Investigaremos las capas de la atmósfera y descubriremos que el clima ocurre principalmente en la capa más baja de la atmósfera. Haremos nuestro propio termómetro para medir la temperatura del aire. También investigaremos cómo se combinan las medidas del tiempo en un mapa meteorológico.

Destrezas del proceso científico

Cuando los científicos **comparan** determinan en qué se parecen y en qué se diferencian dos cosas. Usted puede usar un periódico diario para ayudar a su hijo(a) a comparar las condiciones del tiempo en diferentes áreas del país.

Cada día durante una semana examine la página del tiempo en su periódico local. Observe cómo será el clima en su área y en su estado. Elija un estado o una ciudad que le quede al oeste y compare cada día su clima con el clima de esa localidad. Manténgase informado sobre el clima en las dos localidades. Al final de la semana, vea si puede hallar alguna tendencia. (El clima normalmente se desplaza del oeste al este en Estados Unidos.)

Diversión

El peso del aire presiona todo hacia abajo en la superficie de la Tierra. Esta actividad demuestra uno de los usos diarios de la presión del aire.

Lo que necesitas

- pajita de plástico transparente
- punzón
- frasco de plástico con tapa limpio
- plastilina

Lo que vas a hacer

1. Llena el frasco con agua. Usa la pajita para chupar un poco de agua fuera del frasco.
2. CUIDADO: Pide a un adulto que use un punzón para abrir un hueco a través de la tapa del frasco. El hueco debe ser justo del tamaño de la pajita para que ésta pase.
3. Coloca la pajita a través del hueco. Sella cualquier vacío alrededor de la pajita con plastilina.
4. Trata de chupar agua por la pajita.

Explicación: La presión del aire hace que el agua suba por la pajita. Cuando se sella el frasco, el aire no puede presionar el agua. La pajita no funciona.

Materiales de casa para la actividad

Querido familiar:

Para hacer las actividades en este capítulo, necesitaremos algunos materiales que tal vez tenga en la casa. Observe los artículos de la lista de la derecha. Si es posible, por favor envíe estas cosas con su hijo(a) a la escuela.

¡Gracias por su ayuda y su apoyo!

____ **toallas de papel**
____ **vasitos de papel**
____ **tarjetas**
____ **pajitas de beber transparentes**
____ **plastilina**

Harcourt

School-Home Connection

Chapter Content

In science we are beginning a chapter on Earth and its place in the solar system. We will be studying the nine planets in the solar system, how Earth's tilt causes seasons, and how the sun, moon, and Earth interact to cause the moon's phases and eclipses.

Science Process Skills

For centuries, people have observed the stars. Through careful **observations**, scientists determined that the moon orbits Earth while Earth revolves around the sun. In this activity, you can make your own observations of the moon.

On a clear night, go outside with your child and observe the moon. Take paper, pencil, and a flashlight and draw the shape of the moon. Try to do this every three or four evenings, when fairly clear, for about two weeks. Have your child tell you whether the moon you have traced is either moving toward full moon or toward new moon.

Science Fun

Moonlight is not generated by the moon. Instead, moonlight is reflected sunlight.

What You Need

- flashlight
- small hand mirror
- dark T-shirt

What to Do

1. Put on the shirt. Darken the room.

2. Have your partner shine the light on the front of your shirt. Turn to the left.

3. When you are facing away from the flashlight, hold the mirror to the side of your body. Tilt the mirror until light shines on the dark side of your shirt.

4. Continue turning to the left. Watch how the light changes.

Explanation: In this activity, the light is the sun, the mirror is the moon, and the person in the tee-shirt is Earth. As Earth turns, a spot on the surface moves from day into night. Reflected light from the moon can illuminate the dark side of Earth, but not as much as the sun.

Activity Materials from Home

Dear Family Member:

To do the activities in this chapter, we will need some materials that you may have at home. Please note the items at the right. If possible, please send these things to school with your child.

Your help and support are appreciated!

____ **white paper**
____ **transparent tape**

Harcourt

La escuela y la casa

Contenido del capítulo

Hoy comenzamos un nuevo capítulo de ciencias sobre la Tierra y su lugar en el sistema solar. Estudiaremos los nueve planetas del sistema solar, cómo la inclinación de la Tierra causa las estaciones del año y cómo el Sol, la Luna y la Tierra se afectan entre sí para producir las fases lunares y los eclipses.

Destrezas del proceso científico

Durante siglos, las personas han observado las estrellas. Mediante **observaciones** detalladas, los científicos han determinado que la Luna gira alrededor de la Tierra mientras la Tierra gira alrededor del Sol. En esta actividad puedes hacer tus propias observaciones sobre la Luna.

En una noche despejada, salga con su hijo(a) a observar la Luna. Use un papel, un lápiz y una linterna para dibujar la Luna. Haga esto cada tres o cuatro noches durante dos semanas. Pida a su hijo(a) que indique si los dibujos muestran la Luna avanzando a Luna llena o a Luna menguante.

Diversión

La luz de la Luna no la genera la Luna. En cambio, la luz de la Luna es reflejada por la luz solar.

Lo que necesitas

- linterna
- una camiseta oscura
- un espejo pequeño de mano

Lo que vas a hacer

1. Ponte la camiseta. Oscurece el cuarto.

2. Pide a alguien que alumbre el frente de tu camiseta. Gira a la izquierda.

3. Cuando no estés de cara a la linterna, sostén el espejo al lado de tu cuerpo. Inclina el espejo hasta que la luz se refleje en el lado oscuro de tu camiseta.

4. Continúa girando hacia la izquierda. Observa como cambia la luz.

Explicación: En esta actividad la luz es el Sol, el espejo es la Luna y la persona con la camiseta es la Tierra. Mientras la Tierra gira, una parte de la superficie se mueve del día a la noche. La luz reflejada por la Luna puede iluminar el lado oscuro de la Tierra, pero no tanto como el Sol.

Materiales de casa para la actividad

Querido familiar:

Para hacer las actividades de este capítulo, necesitaremos algunos materiales que tal vez tenga alrededor de la casa. Observe los artículos de la lista de la derecha. Si es posible, por favor envíe estas cosas con su hijo(a) a la escuela.

¡Gracias por su ayuda y apoyo!

____ papel blanco
____ cinta adhesiva transparente

Harcourt

School-Home Connection

Harcourt Science

Chapter Content

Today in science we begin a chapter on the physical properties of matter. We will be examining physical properties—those things that can be observed with the senses. We will see how adding or taking away heat causes it to change state, and we will explore different ways to measure matter.

Science Process Skills

One way we learn about the materials around us is to **measure** them. This activity will give your child practice in making simple measurements of length and volume.

Gather a ruler, measuring cups of different volumes, and several rectangular boxes, such as a CD or audio tape cases and shoe boxes.

- Have your child use the ruler to find the length, width, and height of each of the rectangular objects. Have them estimate each length to the nearest inch or half-inch.

- Have your child identify how much is held by each measuring cup. Challenge him or her to "prove" that two half-cups or four quarter-cups equal one cup.

Science Fun

This activity will give your child practice at describing different physical properties of matter, as well as reinforcing that observations are made using all the senses, not just the eyes.

What You Need

- blindfold
- several pieces of clothing with different textures
- pieces of food with distinct odors, each in a separate plastic bag

What to Do

1. Gather the materials.

2. Give your child each object. Have him or her tell you about the object without looking at it. If your child has trouble, ask questions such as, is it hard or soft? Is it smooth or rough?

3. After your child describes an object, have him or her guess what the object is. Keep track of correct guesses.

Activity Materials from Home

Dear Family Member:

To do the activities in this chapter, we will need some materials that you may have at home. Please note the items at the right. If possible, please send these things to school with your child.

Your help and support are appreciated!

_____ **penny, nickel**
_____ **marble**
_____ **key**
_____ **cotton balls**
_____ **uncooked macaroni**
_____ **twist ties**
_____ **pepper**

Harcourt

La escuela y la casa

Harcourt Ciencias

Contenido del capítulo

Hoy comenzamos un nuevo capítulo de ciencias sobre las propiedades físicas de la materia. Examinaremos las propiedades físicas, esas cosas que se pueden observar con los sentidos. Veremos cómo agregarle o quitarle calor hace que se produzcan cambios en su estado y exploraremos diferentes maneras de medir la materia.

Destrezas del proceso científico

Medir es una manera de aprender sobre los materiales que nos rodean. Esta actividad le dará a su hijo(a) la práctica para hacer medidas sencillas de longitud y volumen.

Busque una regla, tazas de medir de diferentes volúmenes y varias cajas rectangulares como de CD o cintas y cajas de zapatos.

• Pida a su hijo(a) que use la regla para hallar la longitud, el ancho y la altura de cada uno de los objetos rectangulares. Pídale que estime cada longitud a la pulgada o media pulgada más cercana.

• Pida a su hijo(a) que identifique qué cantidad contiene cada taza de medir. Rételo(a) a "comprobar" que dos medias tazas o cuatro cuartos de taza es igual a una taza.

Diversión

Esta actividad le dará a su hijo(a) la práctica para describir diferentes propiedades físicas de la materia así como también reforzará que las observaciones son hechas usando todos los sentidos, no sólo los ojos.

Lo que necesitas

• venda para los ojos

• varios pedazos de tela con diferentes texturas

• pedazos de comida con distintos olores, cada uno en una bolsa de plástico separado

Lo que vas a hacer

1. Recopile con su hijo(a) los materiales.

2. Dé a su hijo(a) cada uno de los objetos. Pídale que le hable del objeto sin mirarlo. Si su hijo(a) tiene problemas, haga preguntas como: ¿Es duro o suave? ¿Es liso o áspero?

3. Después que su hijo(a) describa un objeto, pídale que adivine qué objeto es. Lleve la cuenta de las conjeturas correctas.

Materiales de casa para la actividad

Querido familiar:

Para hacer las actividades de este capítulo, necesitaremos algunos materiales que tal vez tenga en la casa. Observe los artículos de la lista de la derecha. Si es posible, por favor envíe estas cosas con su hijo(a) a la escuela.

¡Gracias por su ayuda y apoyo!

____ **moneda de 1¢, moneda de 5¢**
____ **canica**
____ **llave**
____ **bolitas de algodón**
____ **fideos crudos**
____ **alambritos**
____ **pimienta**

Harcourt

School-Home Connection

Harcourt Science

Chapter Content

In science we are beginning a chapter on how matter changes. We will examine physical changes, such as cutting, folding, and changing state. We will then compare these changes to chemical changes, in which matter is combined and different matter forms.

Science Process Skills

Your child is learning how to **observe** as scientists do. This activity will help your child observe physical changes that occur as you cook a meal.

Have your child help you plan and cook a simple meal such as spaghetti and salad. As you prepare each part of the meal, have your child identify any state changes that occur, such as water changing from a liquid to a gas as the spaghetti water boils. Also have your child discuss how the matter is changed physically as it is prepared. For example, salad ingredients are cut into small pieces, components for salad dressing may be mixed or shaken together, spaghetti changes from something hard to a soft, bendable material.

Science Fun

A mixture is a substance that contains two or more different types of matter. A tossed salad is a common mixture. In this activity, you can reinforce the properties of mixtures, and organize a portion of your home at the same time!

What to Do

1. Identify an area of your home that needs organizing. It may be a play area, a closet, a study area, or the kitchen junk drawer.

2. Work with your child to identify categories of matter to separate from the area. For example, in the kitchen junk drawer, you might wish to separate all the paper clips, rubber bands, and twist ties into separate containers.

3. Continue separating and organizing the parts of the mixture until the area is organized.

Activity Materials from Home

Dear Family Member:

To do the activities in this chapter, we will need some materials that you may have around your home. Please note the items listed at the right. If possible, please send these things to school with your child.

Your help and support are appreciated!

____ **marbles**
____ **rice**
____ **funnel**
____ **cookie sheet**
____ **large glass bowl**
____ **baking soda**
____ **vinegar**

Harcourt

La escuela y la casa

Harcourt Ciencias

Contenido del capítulo

Hoy comenzamos un nuevo capítulo de ciencias sobre cómo cambia la materia. Examinaremos los cambios físicos como cortar, doblar y cambiar de estado. Luego compararemos estos cambios con los cambios químicos, en los cuales la materia se combina y se forman materias diferentes.

Destrezas del proceso científico

Su hijo(a) aprende a **observar** como lo hacen los científicos. Esta actividad ayudará a su hijo(a) a observar los cambios físicos que ocurren mientras usted prepara una comida.

Pida a su hijo(a) que lo ayude a preparar y cocinar una comida sencilla como espaguetis o ensalada. Mientras prepara cada parte de la comida, pida a su hijo(a) que identifique cualquier cambio de estado que ocurra, como el cambio del agua de líquido a gas, mientras el agua de los espaguetis está hirviendo. También pida a su hijo(a) que comente cómo cambia la sustancia físicamente mientras se prepara. Por ejemplo, los ingredientes de la ensalada se cortan en pedazos pequeños, los componentes de los aliños de la ensalada se pueden mezclar o revolver, los espaguetis cambian de algo duro a un material suave que se dobla.

Diversión

Una mezcla es una sustancia que contiene dos o más tipos de materia diferentes. Una ensalada es una mezcla común. En esta actividad, usted puede reforzar las propiedades de las mezclas y organizar una parte de su casa al mismo tiempo.

Lo que vas a hacer

1. Identifique un área de su casa que necesite organizar. Puede ser un área de juego, un armario, un área de estudio o una gaveta de utensilios de cocina.

2. Trabaje con su hijo(a) para identificar categorías de la materia para separar del área. Por ejemplo, en la gaveta de utensilios de cocina, quizás desee separar todos los clips, elásticos y cierres en recipientes separados.

3. Continúe separando y organizando las partes de la mezcla hasta que el área esté organizada.

Materiales de casa para la actividad

Querido familiar:

Para hacer las actividades en este capítulo, necesitaremos algunos materiales que tal vez tenga en la casa. Observe los artículos de la lista de la derecha. Si es posible, por favor envíe estas cosas con su hijo(a) a la escuela.

¡Gracias por su ayuda y su apoyo!

_____ **canicas**
_____ **arroz**
_____ **embudo**
_____ **tazón grande de vidrio**
_____ **bicarbonato**
_____ **vinagre**

Harcourt

School-Home Connection

Harcourt Science

Chapter Content

Our science class is beginning a chapter about energy. We will be learning how energy is stored and used. Our studies will also cover light energy, sound energy, how sound waves move through materials, and how light waves move through some materials as well as through empty space. The chapter ends with a discussion of electricity and how energy changes form.

Science Process Skills

The following activity will help prepare students for classroom discussions of how thermal energy moves. The activity involves the science process skill **hypothesize.** When scientists hypothesize, they make an educated guess based on what they already know. You can give your child practice at making a hypothesis and testing it at breakfast!

Make pancakes. Have your child form a hypothesis about what will happen if he or she puts butter on the pancakes. Ask your child to explain why he or she thought of that hypothesis. Have your child test the hypothesis by putting butter on the pancakes. Talk about how accurate the hypothesis was. Secretly give your child a cold pancake. Repeat the hypothesizing and testing. Compare the results. Discuss why it is important to test a hypothesis.

Science Fun

Lesson 2 in the chapter focuses on how thermal energy moves from place to place. In the activity described below, you can observe the results of radiation, thermal energy that moves without touching anything.

What You Need

- glass jar with lid
- water
- 4 herbal tea bags

What to Do

1. Pour 1 liter (about 4 cups) of water into a glass jar.

2. Add 4 tea bags to the water, and put the lid on the jar.

3. Place the jar in a sunny window.

4. After 3 or 4 hours, observe the jar. You have made sun tea! Add ice and serve in tall glasses.

Activity Materials from Home

Dear Family Member:

To do the activities in this chapter, we will need some materials that you may have around your home. Please note the items at the right. If possible, please send these things to school with your child.

Your help and support are appreciated!

____ **2 clothespins**
____ **rubber bands**
____ **masking tape**
____ **D-cell battery**
____ **miniature light bulb**

Harcourt

La escuela y la casa

Harcourt Ciencias

Contenido del capítulo

Hoy comenzamos a estudiar un capítulo sobre la energía en nuestra clase de ciencias. Vamos a estudiar cómo se utiliza y se almacena la energía. Nuestros estudios también abarcarán la energía de la luz y del sonido, cómo se transfieren las ondas sonoras a través de la materia, y cómo se transfieren las ondas de luz a través de ciertos materiales y a través del espacio vacío. El capítulo finalizará con una conversación sobre la electricidad y cómo la energía se transforma.

Destrezas del proceso científico

La actividad a continuación ayudará a los estudiantes a participar en una discusión sobre cómo se transfiere la energía térmica. Esta actividad requiere una destreza del proceso científico llamada **hacer una hipótesis.** Cuando los científicos hacen una hipótesis, hacen una suposición basada en información que ya poseen. Usted podrá ayudar a su hijo(a) a hacer una hipótesis y a comprobarla mientras desayunan juntos.

Haga panqueques. Invite a su hijo(a) a hacer una hipótesis sobre qué pasaría si pusiera un trozo de mantequilla sobre los panqueques. Anímelo(a) a comprobar su hipótesis poniendo el trozo de mantequilla sobre los panqueques. Hágale notar la precisión de la hipótesis. Sin que se dé cuenta, déle a su hijo(a) un panqueque frío y repita el proceso. Compare ambos resultados. Hable con él o ella sobre por qué es importante comprobar una hipótesis.

Diversión

La lección 2 del capítulo trata sobre cómo la energía térmica se transfiere de un lugar a otro. En la actividad que describimos a continuación, podrás observar los resultados de la radiación, energía térmica que se transfiere sin hacer contacto con nada.

Lo que necesitas

- un frasco de vidrio con su tapa
- agua
- 4 bolsitas de té de hierbas

Lo que vas a hacer

1. Vierte 1 litro (4 tazas) de agua en el frasco de vidrio.

2. Agrégale las 4 bolsitas de té al agua y ponle la tapa.

3. Coloca el frasco en una ventana donde dé bastante sol.

4. Después de 3 ó 4 horas, observa el recipiente. ¡Has hecho tu propio té solar! Pónle hielo y sírvelo en vasos largos.

Materiales de casa para la actividad

Querido familiar:

Para hacer las actividades de este capítulo vamos a necesitar algunos materiales que quizás usted tenga en su casa. Observe la lista de artículos que aparece a la derecha y si le es posible, por favor envíelos con su hijo(a) a la escuela.

¡Gracias por su ayuda y cooperación!

_____ **2 ganchos de ropa**
_____ **bandas elásticas**
_____ **cinta adhesiva**
_____ **pila tamaño "D"**
_____ **bombilla miniatura**

School-Home Connection

Harcourt Science

Chapter Content

Our science class is beginning a chapter on heat. We will learn the difference between heat and thermal energy, we will explore the ways that thermal energy moves, and we will investigate how temperature is measured.

Science Process Skills

A **hypothesis** is an educated guess about what causes an event. It is made based on what is known about the event. Scientists make hypotheses that they can test to learn about the world around them. You can give your child practice at making a hypothesis and then testing it as you eat breakfast!

Make pancakes. Have your child make a hypothesis about what will happen when he or she puts butter on the pancakes. Ask your child to explain why he or she made that hypothesis. Have your child test the hypothesis by putting butter on the cakes. Talk about how accurate the hypothesis was. Secretly give your child a cold pancake. Repeat the hypothesizing and testing, and reviewing. Compare the results. Discuss why it is important to test a hypothesis.

Science Fun

Lesson 2 of this chapter focuses on how thermal energy moves from place to place. In this activity you can observe the results of radiation, thermal energy that moves without touching anything.

What You Need

- glass jar with lid
- water
- 4 herbal tea bags

What to Do

1. Pour 1 liter (about 4 cups) of water into a glass jar.

2. Add 4 tea bags to the water and put the lid on the jar.

3. Place the jar in a sunny window.

4. After 3 or 4 hours, observe the jar. You have made sun tea! Add ice and serve in tall glasses.

Activity Materials from Home

Dear Family Member:

To do the activities in this chapter we will need some materials that you may have at home. Please note the items at the right. If possible, please send these things to school with your child.

Your help and support are appreciated!

___ **metal button**
___ **small pieces of wool**
___ **wooden spoon**
___ **plastic spoons**

La escuela y la casa

Contenido del capítulo

Hoy comenzamos un nuevo capítulo de ciencias sobre el calor. Aprenderemos la diferencia entre calor y energía térmica, exploraremos las formas en que se mueve la energía térmica e investigaremos cómo se mide la temperatura.

Destrezas del proceso científico

Una **hipótesis** es una adivinanza apollada por datos sobre lo que causa un evento. Ésta se hace basada en lo que se conoce sobre el evento. Los científicos formulan hipótesis que pueden comprobar para aprender sobre el mundo que los rodea. ¡Usted puede darle a su hijo(a) práctica para formular una hipótesis y luego probarla mientras toma el desayuno!

Haga panqueques. Pida a su hijo(a) que formule una hipótesis sobre qué pasará cuando coloque mantequilla sobre los panqueques. Pida a su hijo(a) que explique por qué formuló esa hipótesis. Pida a su hijo(a) que compruebe la hipótesis poniendo mantequilla sobre los panqueques. Hable sobre qué tan precisa fue la hipótesis. En secreto, dé a su hijo(a) un panqueque frío. Repita la hipótesis y la prueba. Compare los resultados. Comente por qué es importante comprobar una hipótesis.

Diversión

La Lección 2 de este capítulo enfoca en cómo la energía térmica se mueve de un lugar a otro. En esta actividad puede observar los resultados de la radiación, la energía térmica que se mueve sin tocar nada.

Lo que necesitas

- frasco de vidrio con tapa
- agua
- 4 bolsas de té de hierba

Lo que vas a hacer

1. Coloca 1 litro (casi 4 tazas) de agua en un frasco de vidrio.

2. Agrega 4 bolsas de té al agua y ponle la tapa al frasco.

3. Coloca el frasco donde le dé el Sol.

4. Después de 3 ó 4 horas, observa el frasco. ¡Haz hecho té! Agrégale hielo y sírvelo en un vaso alto.

Materiales de casa para la actividad

Querido familiar:

Para hacer las actividades en este capítulo, necesitaremos algunos materiales que tal vez tenga en la casa. Observe los artículos de la lista de la derecha. Si es posible, por favor envíe estas cosas con su hijo(a) a la escuela.

¡Gracias por su ayuda y su apoyo!

_____ **botón de metal**
_____ **pedazos pequeños de lana**
_____ **cuchara de madera**
_____ **cucharas de plástico**

Harcourt

School-Home Connection

Harcourt Science

Chapter Content

Our science class is beginning a chapter on forces and motion. We will be studying what causes motion and how forces can change the motion of an object. We will also be investigating the scientific definition of *work*. The chapter ends by exploring kinds of simple machines and how they help people do work.

Science Process Skills

Learning how to **interpret data** is a skill in science. When you interpret data, you look at the data and try to find trends.

Set up a simple ramp using a long board. Have your child experiment by rolling a car down the ramp. Have him or her change the height of the ramp (raise or lower), the weight of the cars (tape coins or washers on the cars to increase the weight), or the texture of the ramp (cover with sandpaper or carpet, rub with wax paper). Collect data on the time it takes for the car to roll down the ramp, or how far past the end of the ramp the car travels. After several trials, work with your child to interpret the data. In general, you should find that heavier cars, smoother surfaces, and higher ramps cause faster speeds.

Science Fun

An inclined plane is a flat surface set at an angle to another surface. An inclined plane, such as a ramp, is an example of a simple machine. This activity will help your child explore the uses of this simple machine.

What to Do

Go on a ramp scavenger hunt to see how inclined planes help people do work. Here are some places you might visit:

- Go to the post office to watch how mail is loaded and unloaded.

- Take note of how many intersections have converted the sidewalk-crossing corner into a ramp for wheelchairs.

- Visit libraries, museums, and markets and identify the ramps that allow for wheelchair access.

- Note any ramps being used by people delivering goods from trucks.

When you are finished, analyze the data you gathered. Where are ramps used most often? What is their purpose? Where should ramps be installed?

Activity Materials from Home

Dear Family Member:

To do the activities in this chapter, we will need some materials that you may have at home. Please note the items at the right. If possible, please send these things to school with your child.

Your help and support are appreciated!

____ **string**
____ **wooden board (about 1 m long)**

La escuela y la casa

Harcourt Ciencias

Contenido del capítulo

Hoy comenzamos un nuevo capítulo de ciencias sobre las fuerzas y el movimiento. Estudiaremos lo que causa el movimiento y cómo las fuerzas pueden cambiar el movimiento de un objeto. También investigaremos la definición científica de *trabajo*. El capítulo finaliza explorando los tipos de máquinas sencillas y cómo éstas ayudan a trabajar a las personas.

Destrezas del proceso científico

Aprender cómo **interpretar datos** es una destreza de ciencias. Cuando interpretas datos, miras los datos y tratas de hallar tendencias.

Arme una rampa sencilla usando una tabla larga. Pida a su hijo(a) que experimente rodando un carro por la rampa. Pídale que cambie la altura de la rampa (subir o bajar), el peso de los carros (pegar monedas o tuercas para aumentar el peso) o la textura de la rampa (cubrir con papel de lija o alfombra, frotar con papel encerado). Recopile datos del tiempo que tarda el carro en rodar por la rampa o qué distancia recorre el carro al pasar el final de la rampa. Después de varios intentos, trabaje con su hijo(a) para interpretar los datos. En general, deberían determinar que los carros más pesados, las superficies más lisas y las rampas más altas producen velocidades más rápidas.

Diversión

Un plano inclinado es una superficie plana puesta en un ángulo con otra superficie. Un plano inclinado como una rampa, es un ejemplo de una máquina sencilla. Esta actividad ayudará a su hijo(a) a explorar los usos de esta máquina sencilla.

Lo que vas a hacer

Con su hijo(a), salgan en busca de rampas para determinar cómo los planos inclinados ayudan a trabajar a las personas. Aquí hay algunos lugares que podrían visitar:

- Vayan a la oficina de correos para observar cómo se carga y se descarga el correo.
- Tomen nota de cuántas intersecciones han convertido a la esquina de cruce en una rampa para sillas de rueda.
- Visiten bibliotecas, museos y supermercados e identifiquen las rampas que permiten el acceso a sillas de ruedas.
- Fíjense en cualquier rampa que usan las personas que entregan bienes con camiones.

Cuando terminen, analicen los datos que recopilaron. ¿Dónde se usan las rampas más a menudo? ¿Cuál es su propósito? ¿Dónde se deben instalar las rampas?

Materiales de casa para la actividad

Querido familiar:

Para hacer las actividades en este capítulo, necesitaremos algunos materiales que tal vez tenga en la casa. Observe los artículos de la lista de la derecha. Si es posible, por favor envíe estas cosas con su hijo(a) a la escuela.

¡Gracias por su ayuda y su apoyo!

_____ **hilo**
_____ **tabla de madera**
(casi de 1 m de largo)

Harcourt

TR32 • **Recursos de enseñanza**

Unidad F • **Capítulo 3**

Participating in a School Science Fair

by Barry Van Deman

Science fairs are more than contests for students. They are events that celebrate students' interest and achievement in science. In their first few years of school, students begin to acquire science process skills, such as observing, inferring, measuring, and predicting. Science projects that emphasize these skills are the most appropriate at this stage.

While individual projects at any grade level are fine, whole-class projects or small-group projects are easier to manage and give students experience in working together. In the pages that follow, this guide will focus on small-group and whole-class projects that are completed in the classroom.

The first step to ensure science fair success is to decide on the outcome you want for students and to design projects that will lead them to it. If you want your students to gain skill in observing, inferring, and classifying, you might consider having them do a project that involves collecting objects and sorting them into groups according to observable characteristics. For example, students might collect and sort leaves or observe and classify seashells. Have students record their observations in various ways, such as by drawing, or writing notes or by making a model. These products can be part of a science project display.

The second step to science fair success is to communicate your expectations to students and to their parents or guardians. A letter you can send to parents at the start of the project is included in the following pages. Be sure to keep parents informed as the project progresses.

Finally, keep in mind that working on science fair projects can help your students gain experience in applying science process skills.

A Letter to Family Members

Dear Parent or Guardian,

We will be holding our school science fair on _____.
Participating in a science fair is an enjoyable way for students to apply
science process skills that they have been learning at school.

Our project will focus on the following topic:

_____

_____

Our science fair project will emphasize the following science
process skill(s):

_____

_____

We will be doing one or more group projects at school. Your child
will be part of a project team that will work on a project and display
it at the science fair.

Your child can participate by:

_____

_____

Your can aid your child's success by:

☐ helping complete research

☐ visiting _____

☐ sending in the following supplies: _____

_____

_____

I will be sending home more information about our science
projects and the science fair. If you have any questions, please contact
me at school.

Sincerely,

Ideas for Group Projects

Fuzzy, Hard, and Smooth   Have students find textures in the classroom, at home, and outdoors. Ask them to describe the textures. Groups might display labeled drawings, magazine pictures, photographs, and actual objects.

Shapes All Around Us   Have students find shapes in the classroom, at home, and outdoors. Ask them to identify the shapes. Groups might display labeled pictures and actual objects of various shapes.

Sink or Float   Have students try to float various objects in small tubs of water to see which sink and which float. Groups might display the actual objects, draw them, or show them in a table.

All Kinds of Leaves   Go on a leaf hunt or have students bring leaves they collect near their homes. Have students sort the leaves into groups by characteristics. They might display their groups of leaves by gluing them to poster board and labeling each group by its sorting characteristic.

What Grows from a Seed?   Give each student a dry bean and a paper, plastic, or foam cup filled with potting soil. Have students plant their beans just below the surface of the soil and water them thoroughly (without soaking) each day. Keep the cups near a light source, such as a window. Have students measure, draw, and record their observations daily. Groups might display their plants and charts recording their growth.

What Will a Magnet Pick up (or Attract)?   Give students various metallic and nonmetallic objects and a magnet. Have them test each object to find out if it is attracted to the magnet. For display, group members might draw the objects that are attracted to the magnet on one half of a sheet of poster board and objects that are not attracted on the other half.

How Are Seashells Alike and Different?   Have students sort a collection of seashells into groups by similar characteristics. They might display the unsorted shells along with drawings and descriptions of how they sorted them into groups.

Which Brand of Chocolate Chip Cookies Has the Most Chocolate Chips?   Using at least two brands of cookies, have students carefully break apart cookies and count the number of chocolate chips. Groups can collect the numbers on the chalkboard, and transfer them to poster board for display. They might also want to make graphs using "chocolate chips" made from construction paper.

For additional Science Fair project ideas see pages A1, B1, C1, D1, E1, and F1 in your *Harcourt Science* Teacher's Edition.

Harcourt

Ideas for Displaying Projects

Here are some ideas for displaying student projects in the classroom or at a science fair.

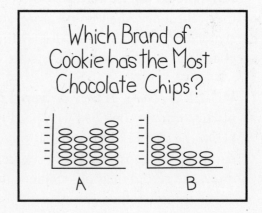

Harcourt

Science Fair Project Planning

Our Science Project Team

Team Members	What will they do?

Harcourt

Name _____ Date _____

Project Results

Our Project

_____

_____

_____

_____

_____

What We Did

_____

_____

_____

_____

_____

What We Found Out

_____

_____

_____

_____

_____

Science Fair

Writing Models

The writing models on the following pages show examples of writing for different purposes. Students can consult these as they complete the Writing Links described in the *Harcourt Science* Pupil Edition or other writing assignments described in the Teacher's Edition. You may wish to distribute copies of the writing models to students or display them on an overhead transparency.

Informative Writing

Persuasive Writing

Narrative Writing

Expressive Writing

Harcourt

Writing in Science

Model: How-To Writing

How-to writing gives directions or explains how to do something. Steps are given in time order.

How to Make Sun Tea

topic sentence

materials needed

You can learn about solar radiation by making sun tea. Plan to make your tea on a warm sunny day. You need a large glass jar with a top and ten tea bags. You also need enough drinking water to fill the jar.

time-order words in steps

Start by filling the jar almost to the top with water. Add the tea bags. Then put the top on the jar. Next, place the jar in the sun. Check on your tea in two hours. You should see that the water is beginning to get darker. After four hours, taste your tea to see if it is ready. If it isn't, keep it in the sun for an hour or two longer. You may need to let your tea cool a bit before you can drink it.

You have made sun tea using radiation from the sun!

Harcourt

Writing in Science

Model: Classification

In a **classification essay,** a writer shows how things can be grouped into categories. Often, examples of each category are provided.

title	**Amphibians and Fish**
topic sentence	Amphibians and fish are animals that live all around us.
first category defined	Amphibians hatch from eggs that are laid in the water. They live in water when they are young. When they are older, they can move onto land. Frogs, toads, and salamanders are all amphibians.
second category defined	Fish are born in water and live their whole lives there. Fish use the gills on the sides of their heads to breathe. They use their fins to move themselves through the water. Salmon, bass, and sharks are fish you might know.

Harcourt

Writing in Science

Model: Research Report

A **research report** provides information about a topic. Reports can be short, or they can be several pages long.

title	**Owls: The Night Hunters**
introduction that identifies topic	Owls are nocturnal. That means owls are most active after dark. The owl's body helps it to hunt at night.
body with detailed information about topic	An owl's eyes are very large. They can see when it is almost totally dark. An owl's eyes cannot move by themselves. An owl looks around by turning its head. Some owls can turn their head almost all the way around!
	Owls have good hearing, too. Their ears are very large. The oval shape of an owl's face helps to send sound to its ears. Also, owls have very soft feathers. Their soft feathers let owls fly silently and surprise their prey.
conclusion	You might be able to see an owl at the zoo. Don't miss seeing these interesting birds!

Harcourt

Writing in Science

Model: Narration

A **narration** presents events in the order in which they occurred. Often, a narration is an eyewitness account of those events.

title	**Water Awareness Week**
topic sentence	We had Water Awareness Week at school last week. We learned how to save water and keep it clean. On Monday we learned that wasting and polluting water means less water for everyone.
events described in time order	On Tuesday and Wednesday, we studied some ways to save water. You can turn off faucets when you brush your teeth. You can take quick showers. You can let the rain water the grass.
	On Thursday, we made posters about saving water. We put the posters up around the school. The best part of the week was Friday. We took a class trip to our town reservoir. We learned how water gets from the reservoir to our houses.
conclusion	Water Awareness Week was fun.

Writing in Science

Model: Explanation

In an **explanation,** the writer helps the reader understand something, such as what something is, how it works, what happens during a process, or why something happens.

title	**How Sedimentary Rocks Are Formed**
topic sentence	Sedimentary rocks are made from particles of minerals or rock. The particles are called sediments. Wind or moving water wears away the sediment from other kinds of rock. When the wind or water slows down, it drops the sediment. The sediment builds up in layers. The layers are usually on the bottom of rivers, lakes, or seas.
body/detailed explanation	Over many years, the weight of the layers makes the sediment harden into rock. This rock is called sedimentary rock. After the rock is formed, wind and water can once again start to wear it away.

Harcourt

Writing in Science

Model: Compare/Contrast

In a **compare-and-contrast essay,** a writer shows how two people, places, or things are alike and how they are different.

title	**Venus and Mars**
topic sentence	The planets closest to Earth are Venus and Mars. They are alike in many ways.
likenesses	Both are called inner planets. They are warmer than the other planets in our solar system because they are closer to the sun. Both Venus and Mars have rocky surfaces. Both planets travel around the sun in regular orbits.
topic sentence	Venus and Mars are different from each other. Venus is much hotter than
differences	Mars because Venus is closer to the sun. Venus orbits the sun in about 225 Earth days. Mars' orbit takes 687 Earth days. You can see the surface of Mars from Earth but Venus is hidden by thick clouds. Venus and Mars rotate in opposite directions. Mars has two moons, but Venus has none.

Writing in Science

Model: Description

A **description** creates a word picture as it tells about one subject. It has a beginning, a middle, and an ending. It includes sensory details.

title	**The Osprey**
beginning that tells what you will describe	I walked down to the lake to fish just after five o'clock one afternoon. A few minutes later I saw the osprey. The bird seemed to come from nowhere. It tucked its reddish wings tightly to its body. Then it dove toward the sparkling water.
middle with sensory details	Just before hitting the surface, the osprey opened its huge wings. It plunged its sharp claws under the water with a splash. Slowly, the bird rose from the water with a large fish grasped in its claws. I did not catch any fish myself that day. But the picture of the osprey will stay in my mind forever.
ending	

Harcourt

Writing in Science

Model: Opinion

An **opinion essay** has a beginning, a middle with paragraphs supporting the writer's opinion, and an ending that restates the opinion.

title	**Recycling Is Best**
beginning with opinion stated	Some people think that it's best to get rid of trash by burning it to produce energy. I think recycling is a much better idea.
middle with reasons to support opinion	Burning trash can provide energy, but it also causes air pollution. The smoke from burning trash can contain chemicals that pollute the air. If newspaper and plastic bottles are burned, new paper and plastic must be made. This causes even more pollution.
ending with restated opinion or request for action	Recycling causes less pollution than making new products. It even saves energy. That means less pollution for everyone. This is why I think that recycling is better than burning trash.

Writing in Science

Model: Request

To **request** information or products from a company, use a business-letter format. A business letter has the same parts as a friendly letter, plus an inside address. It also uses formal language.

heading

426 Harris Avenue
Jamaica Plain, MA 02130
April 8, 2001

inside address

Ms. Nancy MacAllister
Broward Observatory
2135 Ridge Road
Williamstown, MA 01267

greeting

Dear Ms. MacAllister:

statement of request and supporting reasons

Our third grade class at Leighton Elementary School has been studying astronomy. We would like to take a tour of the Broward Observatory.

We began learning about our solar system last September. Touring the observatory would let us see how astronomers work. Using your telescope, we could get a good look at some of the planets we have been studying.

Our class can visit any time in May. Thank you for your help.

closing

Sincerely,

signature

Aaron Bishop

Writing in Science

Model: Business Letter

In a **business letter** a writer uses formal language to ask for or share information, to request something, or to praise or complain about a product or service. It has the same parts as a friendly letter, plus an inside address.

heading

776 Main Street
Allegheny, NY 14706
September 15, 2001

inside address

Mr. Robert B. Davies, Director
Wind Power Institute
630 Elm Street
Madison, WI 53706

greeting

Dear Mr. Davies:

body

Our third grade class at Harris Elementary School is learning about renewable energy. We hope that the Wind Power Institute will help us learn more about wind power.

We read about your video "Clean Power, Wind Power." I am sending a money order for $17.95 for the video. Please send it to us as soon as possible.

We are glad to have a chance to learn more about wind power. Thank you for your help.

closing

Sincerely,

signature

Carl Olson

Writing in Science

Model: Story

Every **story** has a setting (time and place), one or more characters, and a series of events called a plot. A plot has a beginning, a middle, and an end.

title

beginning: introduce the setting and the characters

middle: a plot with a problem to solve

end: the problem is solved

The Volcano

Robert couldn't believe what he was seeing. The instruments said that the volcano was ready to erupt. There was no time to waste.

Robert ran to his truck and drove toward the state forest. Hundreds of people were camped there for the weekend. They had no idea the beautiful mountain at the center of the park was about to explode.

Robert reached the forest just as the ground began to shake. He went from camp to camp warning everyone. By then black smoke drifted from the mountain top. But Robert kept the campers from panicking. At 1 P.M., the volcano erupted, destroying the entire state forest. But thanks to Robert, all of the campers had escaped.

Writing in Science

Model: Personal Story

A **personal story** is told in the first person. Someone or something is telling the story, using pronouns such as *I, my,* and *me.* Like any story, there is a beginning, a middle, and an end.

title	**My Blizzard Adventure**
beginning: the narrator is identified	I have lived in San Antonio, Texas my whole life and I had never seen snow. I was excited to visit my cousins in Michigan for Christmas. I hoped for snow, but none fell until our last morning there. When I woke up and looked out the window, I couldn't believe my eyes! The ground was white. Huge snowflakes were falling.
middle: the narrator tells a series of events	My uncle Manny drove us to the airport to catch our flight home. Strong winds blew the snow all around. When we finally arrived, we learned that our flight wouldn't be able to leave until the storm was over. We spent twenty hours at the airport until the weather cleared.
end: the narrator wraps up the story	When we finally arrived in San Antonio, it was amazing to find hot sun and clear pavement. It was as if my adventure in the blizzard had been a dream. But I know it wasn't. I have the photos to prove it!

Writing in Science

Model: Poem

A **poem** uses rhythm and language that appeals to the senses to paint a "word picture" for the reader. Some poems have rhyming lines, but some poems do not.

title	Hot Stuff
"word pictures" that help the reader picture what the poem is about	To move thermal energy From place to place Put a conductor In the space. To keep heat from moving Nothing works greater Than filling the space With an insulator.

Writing in Science

Model: Friendly Letter

In a **friendly letter**, a person writes to someone he or she knows. A friendly letter has a heading, a greeting, a body, a closing, and a signature. In the heading, include a comma between the city and state, and between the day of the month and the year.

heading (writer's address and date)

412 East Houston St.
San Antonio, TX 78205
May 15, 2001

greeting

Dear Suzanne,

body

I can't wait to visit you at the farm again. Remember how much fun we had the last time? I really loved helping to harvest the vegetables. Those cucumbers were the best!

This spring, my family decided to plant our own garden in the backyard. It's really tiny compared to your farm!

We even started a compost pile in the backyard. Now instead of throwing our vegetable scraps away, we compost them. Later, we'll add the compost to our garden. Maybe by the time you visit we'll have some cucumbers of our own!

closing

Your friend,

signature

Angela

Harcourt

Picture Cards

Card #1
Canada goose

Card #2
albatross chick

Card #3
hermit crab

Card #4
armadillo

Harcourt

Picture Cards

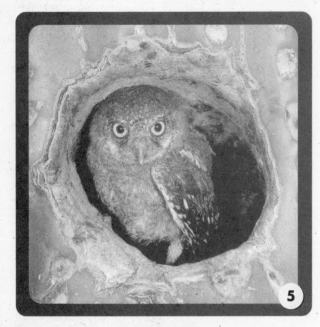

Card #5
elf owl

Card #6
gray foxes

Card #7
prairie dog

Card #8
snakes

Harcourt

Picture Cards

Card #9
bees

Card #10
termites and a termite mound

Card #11
bats

Card #12
beaver

Picture Cards

Card #13
osprey

Card #14
young polar bear

Card #15
newt

Card #16
oysters on mangrove roots

Harcourt

Picture Cards

Card #17
wasps

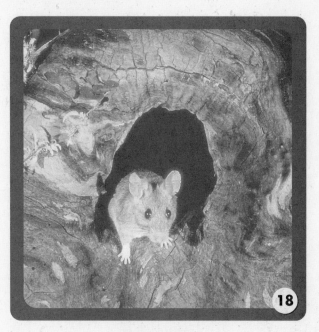

Card #18
wood rat

Card #19
mountain lion

Card #20
eel in coral

Harcourt

Picture Cards

Card #21
rock quarry with blocks of marble

Card #22
oil derrick

Card #23
tilled field

Card #24
forest

Picture Cards

Card #25
iron ore

Card #26
marble statues

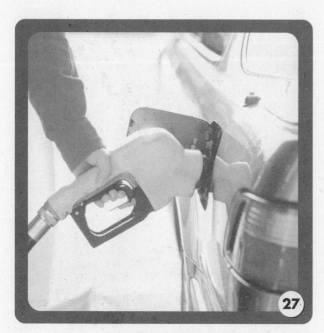

Card #27
car being filled at gasoline pump

Card #28
corn

Harcourt

Picture Cards

Card #29
wooden house frames

Card #30
steel bridge

Card #31
gravel road

Card #32
garden path

Harcourt

Picture Cards

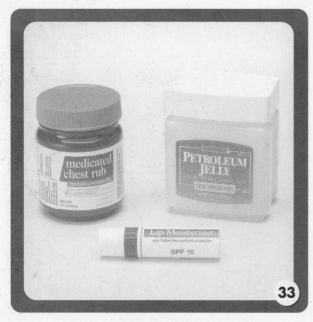

Card #33
personal care products

Card #34
plastic sports equipment

Card #35
blue jeans, cotton balls, towels

Card #36
flowers

Picture Cards

Card #37
furniture

Card #38
notebook

Card #39
iron fence

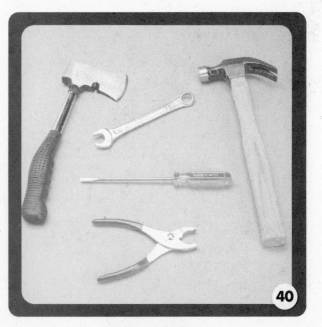

Card #40
tools

Harcourt

Picture Cards

Card #41
Mercury

Card #42
Venus

Card #43
Earth

Card #44
Mars

Picture Cards

Card #45
Jupiter

Card #46
Saturn

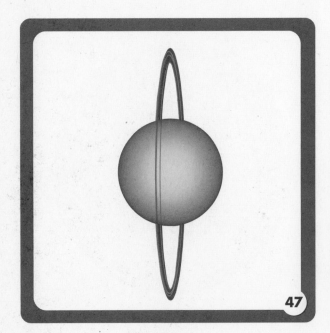

Card #47
Uranus

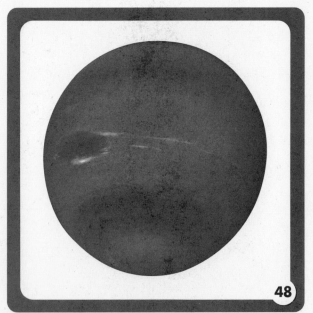

Card #48
Neptune

Harcourt

Picture Cards

Card #49
Pluto

Name _____ Date _____

ACTIVITIES FOR HOME OR SCHOOL

WHAT STEMS DO

How does water move through a stem?

Materials

- 3 1-L plastic bottles
- water
- food coloring
- 3 freshly cut white carnations
- scissors

Procedure

❶ Fill the plastic bottles with water. Add a few drops of food coloring. Put a different color in each bottle.

❷ **CAUTION** **Be careful when using scissors.** Trim the end off the stem of each flower. Place one flower in each bottle.

❸ Keep the flowers in the bottles overnight. Then observe the flowers.

Draw Conclusions

Explain your observations. Make a bouquet of flowers with the colors you like best.

GROWING PLANTS

Can plant parts be used to grow a new plant?

Materials

- 1 plant with many stems and leaves
- scissors
- 1-L plastic bottle
- water
- ruler

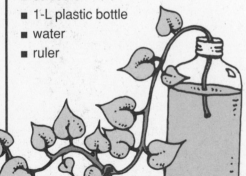

Procedure

❶ **CAUTION** **Be careful when using scissors.** Cut off a 15-cm piece of the plant.

❷ Fill the plastic bottle with water. Place the cut part of the plant in the bottle.

❸ Place the plant in bright sunlight.

Draw Conclusions

Observe the plant for ten days. Record any changes you observe.

A35

Harcourt

ACTIVITIES FOR HOME OR SCHOOL

SHELL STUDY

Why is a spiral shell larger at one end?

Materials

- safety goggles
- gloves
- spiral shell from an animal such as a whelk, conch, or sea snail
- coarse sandpaper
- hand lens

Procedure

1. **CAUTION** **Put on the safety goggles and gloves.** Observe the outside of the shell. Rub the tip of the shell with sandpaper until you have a hole about 5 millimeters (about $\frac{1}{4}$ in.) wide.

2. Use the hand lens to observe the inside of the shell. What do you see?

Draw Conclusions

Animals that live in spiral shells usually keep their shells for their whole lives. When they begin their lives, they are very small. Their shells are very small too.

Think about the shell you observed. Why do you think the spiral is small at one end and gets bigger at the other end?

FEATHER STUDY

What are the parts of feathers?

Materials

- 1 or 2 types of feathers from a bird
- hand lens

Procedure

1. Study the feathers. Use the hand lens to look at their parts. Record what you observe.

2. Touch the feathers as you look at them. Record what you feel.

Draw Conclusions

Discuss what you know about birds. Think of ways the feathers help birds fly.

A85

Harcourt

Name _____ Date _____

ACTIVITIES FOR HOME OR SCHOOL

EARTHWORM HABITAT

What is the habitat of an earthworm?

Materials

- clear plastic container
- garden soil (not potting soil)
- 2 to 3 earthworms
- small rocks, sticks, and leaves
- wax paper
- water

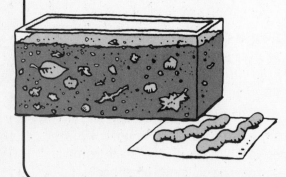

Procedure

1. Loosely spread the soil on the wax paper. Add the rocks, sticks, and leaves. Add a small amount of water so the soil is moist but not wet. Mix these materials together.

2. Add the soil mixture to the plastic container. Carefully add the earthworms to the loose soil. Place your earthworm habitat in a warm, dark place. Keep the soil moist.

Draw Conclusions

After observing your earthworm habitat for a week, make a list of the things you think the habitat you provided gave your earthworms that they needed to live.

SALT WATER AND FRESH WATER

How are salt water and fresh water different?

Materials

- small jar
- small spoon
- water
- salt
- egg in the shell

Procedure

1. Half fill the jar with water. Put the egg in the jar. Record what happens to the egg.

2. Remove the egg, and stir a spoonful of salt into the water. Put the egg back into the water, and record what happens to the egg.

3. Continue adding salt to the water until you observe a change.

Draw Conclusions

How do you think salt in the water affects the animals living in the ocean?

B43

ACTIVITIES FOR HOME OR SCHOOL

FOOD CHAINS

How do animals get their food?

Materials
- name tags
- colored game markers
- small plastic bags

Procedure
Play this game with ten or more people.

1 Have each player wear a tag that names him or her as a grasshopper, a snake, or a hawk. Scatter the game markers over a large area. The game markers are food.

2 Each round of the game is 30 seconds. In the first round, only grasshoppers play. They collect as many markers as they can and put them in their bags.

3 In the next round, only snakes play.

4 In the final round, only hawks play.

Draw Conclusions
Which animals had the most food after three rounds? Talk about your answer.

ENERGY FLOW

How does energy flow through a food chain?

Materials
- index cards
- crayons
- pushpins
- yarn

Procedure
1 Divide the class into five groups: producers, plant eaters, plant and animal eaters, animal eaters, and decomposers.

2 Have each person in your group draw on an index card and label a kind of plant or animal that is from your group.

3 Form teams made up of one member from each group. Each team should make a food chain with the pictures. Use yarn to connect the parts on a bulletin board.

Draw Conclusions
How does energy flow through the food chain?

B69

Harcourt

Use with page B69.

Name _____ Date _____

ACTIVITIES FOR HOME OR SCHOOL

STREAK

What color streak do some minerals have?

Materials
- streak plate or piece of tile
- minerals common to your area, such as chalcopyrite, hematite, pyrite, talc, gypsum, sphalerite, muscovite, galena, fluorite, and calcite

Name of Mineral	Color of Mineral	Color of Streak

Procedure
1. Make a chart like the one shown.
2. Make a mark on the tile with the first mineral. Record the color of the mark it makes. The mark is called the streak.
3. Repeat step 2 for each mineral. Record your results.

Draw Conclusions
Compare the color of the minerals with the color of the streaks. Are they the same? How could streaks help you identify minerals that may look alike?

MINERALS IN SAND

What minerals are found in sand?

Materials
- sand
- sheet of paper
- hand lens
- toothpick
- mineral descriptions

Procedure
1. Spread the sand on a sheet of paper.

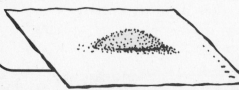

2. Observe the colors and shapes of the sand grains with the hand lens. Each type of mineral grain has a different color and shape.
3. Use the toothpick to move the grains of each mineral into a separate pile.

Draw Conclusions
Identify the minerals. Use the descriptions your teacher gives you. Which mineral is the most common?

C27

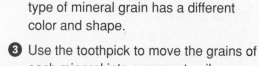

Harcourt

ACTIVITIES FOR HOME OR SCHOOL

SHAKE THE EARTH

What are some effects of earthquakes?

Materials

- baking pan filled with gelatin
- plastic wrap
- large croutons

Procedure

❶ Cover the top of the gelatin with plastic wrap.

❷ Use croutons to make buildings on top of the gelatin.

❸ Move the pan up and down. Then move the pan from side to side. Then tap one end of the pan as you move it. Observe the movement of the gelatin.

Draw Conclusions

Did the movement damage your buildings? **Record** your observations. How is this model like an earthquake?

WEATHERING

Can chemicals in water wear away rock?

Materials

- 6 small glass jars without labels
- wax pencil
- 3 types of rock chips (limestone, sandstone, quartzite)
- water
- white vinegar

Procedure

❶ Label two jars *limestone*. Write *sandstone* on two jars. Write *quartzite* on the last two jars.

❷ Put a few rock chips in each jar. Make sure the chips match the jar's label.

❸ Fill one jar of each pair with water. Fill the other jar with vinegar.

❹ Observe what happens. Wait 30 minutes, and observe again. Let the jars sit overnight. Then, observe them again.

Draw Conclusions

How did the vinegar and the water affect the rocks?

C55

Name _____ Date _____

SOIL AND PLANTS

How does soil help plants grow?

Materials

- 4 plants of the same kind
- potting soil
- sand
- water
- measuring cup
- ruler

Procedure

1. Take the plants from their store pots. Dump out the soil. Rinse the roots.

2. Put each plant back into its empty pot. Put potting soil around two plants. Put sand around the other two plants. Water each plant with the same amount of water.

3. Put the plants in the same sunny place. Use the measuring cup to give the plants the same amount of water each day.

4. Observe the plants for 14 days. Measure their heights. Count the leaves.

Draw Conclusions

Which soil is best for growing the plants?

FOOD FROM SOIL

Where do the foods you eat come from?

Materials

- outline map of the United States
- an encyclopedia
- crayons or colored pencils

Procedure

1. Get a map of the United States from your teacher.

2. Make a list of some of the foods you like to eat. Find out where these foods are grown. Look up the information in an encyclopedia.

3. Use the map to share your findings. Draw a picture of each food on your list. Glue each picture onto the map to show where the food is grown.

Draw Conclusions

Where do the foods you eat come from?

C81

Harcourt

ACTIVITIES FOR HOME OR SCHOOL

HOW MUCH WASTE?

How much waste does your class throw away each day?

Materials
- paper
- pencil

What We Threw Away Today	
Newspaper and Magazines	
Cardboard and Other Paper	
Glass Containers	
Plastic Containers	
Plastic Wrapping and Bags	
Other	

Procedure
1. Copy one chart for the class. Put the chart and a pencil next to the trash can.

2. All students in your class should record what they throw away. If a paper is thrown away, then a *1* is written in the Paper row. If 3 plastic bottles are thrown away, then *3 bottles* is written in the Plastic Containers row.

Draw Conclusions
After gathering data for one day, total all the things that were thrown away. How could your class recycle more?

REUSE IT!

How can some classroom materials be reused?

Materials
- large cardboard or plastic boxes
- black marking pen
- tape

Procedure
1. Use the chart from "How Much Waste?" As a class, decide which materials could be reused instead of being thrown away. Work with your teacher to find a place in the room to store materials that can be reused.

2. Find cardboard boxes or plastic bins for keeping the materials. Label each box with the material it will hold. Be sure that items that had food in them, such as plastic containers, are rinsed before being put in the boxes.

Draw Conclusions
After you have started your REUSE IT! center, check your trash again. How does the amount of trash compare with the amount of trash before the REUSE IT! center was started?

C109

Harcourt

ACTIVITIES FOR HOME OR SCHOOL

CLOUD IN A JAR

How do raindrops form?

Materials
- metal pie pan
- freezer
- glass jar without lid
- hot water
- ice cubes

Procedure

❶ Put the pan in the freezer for an hour.

❷ Just before you take the pan out, have your teacher fill the jar halfway with hot water.

❸ Remove the pan from the freezer, and fill it with ice cubes. Place the pan on top of the jar. Leave it there for a few minutes.

Draw Conclusions
Observe what happens inside the jar. How is this like part of the water cycle?

MAKING RAINDROPS

Why do raindrops fall?

Materials
- dropper
- water
- clear plastic coffee-can lid
- pencil

Procedure
❶ Fill the dropper with water.

❷ Turn the lid so the top of the lid rests flat on the table. Drop small drops of water onto the lid. Put as many drops as you can on the lid without having the drops touch.

❸ Quickly turn the lid over.

❹ Holding the lid upside down, move drops together with the pencil point. What happens?

Draw Conclusions
How is this similar to what happens in clouds?

D23

Harcourt

ACTIVITIES FOR HOME OR SCHOOL

MEASURE PRECIPITATION

How can you find out how much rain falls?

Materials
- masking tape
- ruler
- clear plastic 1-L bottle with top cut off

Procedure

1 Tape the ruler to the outside of the bottle. The 1-in. mark should be at the bottom of the bottle.

2 Put your rain gauge outside before it rains. Do not place it under a tree or under an object that might block the rain.

3 Check the amount of water in the bottle after the rain stops.

Draw Conclusions
Look on the weather page of the newspaper. How much rain fell the day you used your gauge? Was your measurement correct? How close was your measurement?

MEASURE THE WIND

How fast does the wind blow?

Materials
- 2 cardboard strips
- stapler
- cap of a ballpoint pen
- 4 small paper cups (3 white, 1 red)
- watch with second hand
- scissors
- wire

Procedure

1 Make an X with the cardboard strips. Staple the strips together.

2 Use the scissors to make a hole in the middle of the X. Push the pen cap into the hole as shown.

3 Cut a slit in the opposite sides of each cup. Attach the cups as shown.

4 Push the piece of wire deep into the ground outside. Balance the pen cap on the wire.

5 Count the times the red cup spins by in 1 minute. Divide this number by 10. The answer tells how many miles per hour the wind is blowing.

Draw Conclusions
Measure the speed of the wind over the next several days. How does the speed change?

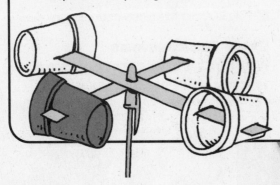

D51

Harcourt

Name _____ Date _____

EARTH MODEL

Why do we have seasons?

Materials

- Styrofoam ball
- flashlight
- two pencils

Procedure

❶ Stick a pencil through the middle of the ball. This represents Earth's axis.

❷ With the other pencil, draw a line around the middle of the ball. This is

the equator. Put the Earth on a table. The axis should lean to the right.

❸ Shine the flashlight on the left side of the Earth. The light represents the sun. Place the light about 13 cm away. Observe where the light rays hit the ball.

❹ Shine the light on the right side of the Earth. Where do the light rays hit the ball? Compare how the light hits the ball each time.

Draw Conclusions

How does this explain seasons in the northern half of the Earth?

A LOOK AT ROTATION

How does day become night?

Materials

- a small self-stick note
- spinning Earth globe
- flashlight

Procedure

❶ Write where you live on the self-stick note. Place the note on your state on the globe.

❷ Shine the flashlight on the globe. Your teacher will then turn off the lights.

❸ Slowly spin the globe counterclockwise.

Draw Conclusions

What happens to the place where you put your note? What does this represent?

D85

Harcourt

Name _____ Date _____

PROPERTIES OF METALS

Which metals have magnetic properties?

Materials

- magnet
- penny
- piece of aluminum foil
- straight pin
- scissors
- dime
- paper clip

	Objects
Magnetic	
Non-Magnetic	Objects

Procedure

1. Copy the chart onto a sheet of paper.

2. Place the magnet close to the penny. Does the penny stick to the magnet? Write down the results on your chart.

3. Repeat Step 2 for each of the other objects. Write down the results for each one on the chart.

Draw Conclusions

Study your completed chart. Are all metals attracted by a magnet? Which kinds are?

MASS OF LIQUIDS

Which of three liquids has the greatest mass?

Materials

- clear measuring cup
- water
- oil
- red vinegar

Procedure

1. Will water float on oil? Or will oil float on water? Predict which liquid will float on the other.

2. Pour some water into the measuring cup.

3. Add some oil. Observe what happens to the oil. Write down your observations. Was your prediction correct?

4. Will the vinegar float on the water? Make a prediction.

5. Pour some red vinegar into the measuring cup. Let it stand still for five minutes. Write down your observations.

Draw Conclusions

The lightest liquid floats on the others. List the liquids from lightest to heaviest.

E33

Harcourt

Name _____ Date _____

ACTIVITIES FOR HOME OR SCHOOL

CHANGES IN COOKING

What happens to muffins as they bake?

Materials

- 1 box of muffin mix
- other needed ingredients
- mixing bowl
- spoon
- muffin pan

Procedure

❶ Read and follow the directions on the box of muffin mix.

❷ Halfway through the cooking time, open the oven or turn on the oven light and observe the muffins. Record your observations.

Draw Conclusions

What is happening to the muffins?

MAKING A SOLUTION

Which works better, hot water or cold water?

Materials

- 2 small, heat-proof glass containers
- cold water
- spoon
- sugar
- clock with second hand
- warm water (from the tap)

Procedure

❶ Fill one container with cold water.

❷ Mix a spoonful of the sugar into the water. Stir until the sugar dissolves.

❸ Watch the clock to see how long it takes. Record the number of seconds it takes.

❹ Repeat Steps 1–3 using warm water.

Draw Conclusions

How were the results different? Why do you think they were different?

E53

Harcourt

Name _____ Date _____

ACTIVITIES FOR HOME OR SCHOOL

HOT ICE

What environments make ice cubes melt fastest?

Materials
- 3 ice cubes of equal size
- 3 foam cups

Procedure
❶ Place one ice cube in each cup.

❷ Choose three different places to leave the cups. Predict which ice cube will melt most during a half-hour.

❸ Place the cups in their locations. Thirty minutes later, get the cups and observe the ice cubes.

❹ Which ice cube melted the most? Did your results support your hypothesis?

Draw Conclusions
How did heat affect your ice cubes?

SUNNY WINDOW   BOOKCASE   CLOSET

BIG EARS

How do big ears help animals hear?

Materials
- sheet of plain paper

Procedure
❶ Work with a partner for this activity. Standing about 3 meters from your partner, have him or her whisper something to you. Can you hear what he or she said?

❷ Now roll your sheet of paper into a cone, and hold the small end to your ear. Have your partner whisper at the same level as before. Were you able to hear your partner better this time?

Draw Conclusions
Explain how you think the cone helped you hear the whispering better. Use the term *sound waves* in your explanation.

ACTIVITIES FOR HOME OR SCHOOL

TESTING INSULATORS

Is wool or sand a better insulator?

Materials

- 1 small coffee can with plastic lid
- 2 wool socks
- scissors
- 1 long lab thermometer
- clock with a second hand
- hair dryer
- 3 cups of sand

Procedure

❶ Stuff the can with the socks. Put the lid on. Cut a small hole in the middle of the lid for the thermometer. Make sure the thermometer is surrounded by wool. After five minutes, read and record the temperature.

❷ Start the hair dryer. Warm the outside of the can. Watch the thermometer and the clock. See how long it takes the temperature to go up 10°C.

❸ Repeat using sand in the coffee can.

Draw Conclusions

Compare results. Which is the better insulator? How do you know?

COOLING WATER

How long does it take for warm water to cool?

Materials

- 2 foam cups
- measuring cup
- 2 thermometers
- clock with a second hand
- warm water

Procedure

❶ Fill one cup with 1 cup of warm water. Fill the other cup with $\frac{1}{2}$ cup of warm water.

❷ In which cup will the water cool faster? Make a hypothesis to answer the question. Write down your hypothesis.

❸ Make a chart to record temperatures. Record the starting temperature in each cup. Then record the temperature of each cup every minute until one cup of water reaches room temperature.

Draw Conclusions

Was your hypothesis correct? Explain.

F59

Harcourt

Use with page F59.

ACTIVITIES FOR HOME OR SCHOOL

MOVEMENT FROM AIR

How can you move a Ping Pong ball with your breath?

Materials
- Ping Pong ball
- 3 straws
- colorful tape

Procedure
❶ Work in groups of three. Each person needs a straw. Clear a space on the floor. With tape, mark a course on the floor. Make sure the course has some twists and turns in it.

❷ Put the Ping Pong ball at the beginning of the course. With your partners, blow on the ball to make it follow the path.

Draw Conclusions
From which angle did you blow to make the ball move farthest? Which made the ball move farther, blowing softly or blowing hard? Which made the ball move farther, blowing steadily or blowing in short puffs?

MEASURING WEIGHT

How can you make your own spring scale?

Materials
- paper cup
- a large, heavy rubber band
- 2 rulers   ■ tape
- string   ■ objects

Procedure
❶ With your pencil, punch two small holes on each side of the paper cup. Place the rubber band as shown. Thread a piece of string through each pair of holes in the cup and tie the cup to the rubber band.

❷ Hold the ruler straight, and have your partner use another ruler to measure the length of the rubber band from the top of the cup to the ruler.

❸ Compare the weights of different objects by putting them in the cup and measuring the length of the rubber band.

Draw Conclusions
How is the length of the rubber band related to the weight of the objects put in the cup?

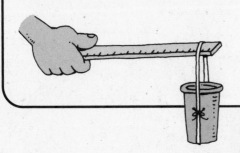

F85

Vocabulary Activities

The word cards on pages TR91–130 contain all the glossary words for Grade 3. The activities listed here suggest ways to use the word cards to do the following:

- increase students' understanding of science terms and concepts.
- help students develop their decoding (phonics and structural analysis) skills.
- meet the individual needs of your classroom.

Concept Activities

1. Categories

Grouping: Whole class or large group; pairs (Challenge)

Materials: word cards; paper and pencil (Challenge)

Have students work with words that are clearly related, either looking for words that fit categories, identifying categories, or creating categories. Here are some examples.

Categories	Vocabulary Words
Layers of Earth	mantle, crust, core
Objects in Space	comet, planet, star
Parts of Plants	leaf, root, stem
Types of Rocks	igneous rock, metamorphic rock, sedimentary rock
Kinds of Animals, Living Things	amphibian, mammal, reptile
Landforms	canyon, plateau, valley
Forms of Matter	liquid, gas, solid

"The words are gills, scales, fins"

"Parts of a Fish!"

Easy: Give students the category and help them search through the word cards to find words that fit.

Average: Give students three vocabulary words and have them decide what category best describes all three.

Challenge: Have student partners identify their own sets of word cards and categories. Provide time for partners to challenge other pairs to match words and categories. Give them the option of adding a non-vocabulary word to fill out a category.

Harcourt

2. Antonym Antics

Grouping: Whole class or large group

Materials: word cards; drawing materials (Easy and Challenge)

Before beginning the activity, separate pairs of antonyms from the word cards. Start by discussing what antonyms are (words with opposite meanings), using common opposites such as *hard* and *easy*, *tall* and *short*, *day* and *night*.

Easy: Display pairs of antonyms. Discuss how the two words in each set differ in meaning. Then have students choose a pair to illustrate, showing in the drawing how opposite the words are in meaning. Ask students to share their drawings.

Average: Add 6 word cards to the deck as distracters. Then select a word card that has an opposite and talk about the word's meaning. Have students find a word that is an antonym. Discuss how these two words differ.

Challenge: Have students look through the word cards for a word that they can name an antonym for. Tell them that they can match up word cards or match a word card with a word they know. Ask students to write a description for each set of opposites without using either word. Have them exchange descriptions with a partner and challenge the partner to identify the words described.

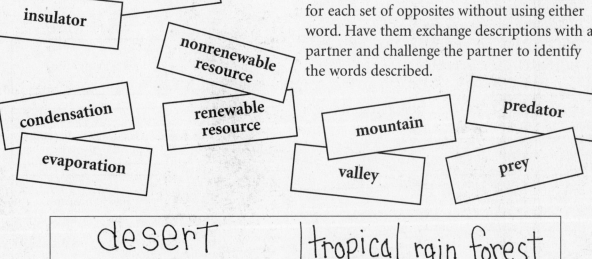

Harcourt

Vocabulary Activities

3. Word Definition Map

Grouping: Whole class or large group; small group (Average); pairs (Challenge)

Materials: word cards, chalk; paper and pencil (Average and Challenge)

Have students explore certain words in depth. Have them use a Word Definition Map to examine a word's definition, its characteristics, and some examples related to the word. On the board, draw a map like the one shown below. Go over the format with students, using the vocabulary word *mammal*.

Easy: Erase the example word and its related text. Work with students to fill in Word

Definition maps for one or two of these words: *amphibian, reptile, constellation, forest, planet, rock.*

Average: Divide students into small groups. List these words on the board: *amphibian, reptile, constellation, forest, planet, rock.* Have each group pick a word and fill out a Word Definition map. Provide sharing time.

Challenge: Pair students up, and have each pair select one or two vocabulary words to explore, filling out a Word Definition map for each word. Provide time for students to share their completed maps.

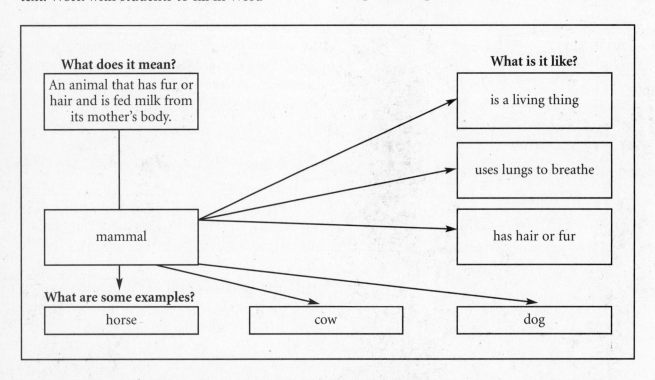

What does it mean?
An animal that has fur or hair and is fed milk from its mother's body.

What is it like?
is a living thing

uses lungs to breathe

has hair or fur

mammal

What are some examples?
horse   cow   dog

4. Crossed Words

Grouping: Whole class or large group (Easy), Pairs (Average and Challenge)

Materials: word cards, chalk, paper and pencil (Average and Challenge)

Have students create a simplified word puzzle with vocabulary words as entries. In these puzzles, a central "starter" vocabulary word is listed

vertically. A vocabulary word that shares the first letter is written horizontally, then one that shares the second letter, and so on. Clues are written for the Starter Word and for each numbered word. Go over the format with students, using *root* as a starter word.

Harcourt

Starter Word Clue: What is the part of a plant that is under the ground?

1. o r b i t
2. c o r e
3. f l o o d
4. h e a t

1. path of a planet as it revolves around the sun
2. center of Earth
3. great flow of water over land
4. transfer of thermal energy from a piece of matter to another

Easy: Work with students to create a crossed-words puzzle on the board. Help them look through their word cards for a good four- or five-letter starter word, let them find words that share common letters, and work with them to create clues.

Average: Have students work in small groups to make their own puzzle, using a four- or five-letter starter word of their choice.

Challenge: Have students work in small groups to make their own puzzle. Tell them to select a longer vocabulary word, such as *germinate*, to be the starter word.

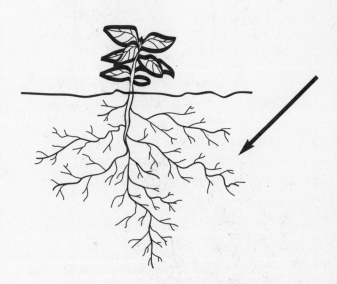

5. Mixed Meanings

Grouping: Whole class or large group (Easy), small group (Average and Challenge)

Materials: word cards, chalk, *Harcourt Science* glossary, dictionary; paper and pencil (Average and Challenge)

Have students work with words that have meanings other than their glossary definitions. Use the word *star* as an example, contrasting the glossary definition ("a hot ball of glowing gases") with the concept of a movie star. List these vocabulary words on the board: *conductor, plain, rock, root, scales, stem.*

Easy: For each word, have students find and dictate the glossary definition. Write it on the board. Ask students to give any other meanings

they know for the word. Then have them take turns finding the word in the dictionary and reading out other definitions. Help them pick a contrasting definition, and write it on the board. Have students suggest context sentences for each meaning of the word.

Average: Have students work in small groups, writing down the glossary definition of a word, finding a contrasting dictionary definition, and coming up with context sentences. Give them a chance to share their work.

Challenge: Use the procedure described in "Average," but challenge students to come up with a single context sentence that includes the contrasting meanings for a word (For example: The movie <u>stars</u> looked up at the <u>stars</u>.)

6. Hidden Words

Grouping: Whole class or large group (Easy), small group (Average), pairs (Challenge)

Materials: word cards, chalk; paper and pencil (Average and Challenge)

Vocabulary words can be hidden inside sentences, with hints given to point toward the hidden words. Write this sentence and hint on the board:

Mitch eats ice cream. (Hint: It moves from a hot place to a cold place.)

Help students use the hint as they look through their word cards to find the word *heat*. Underline it (Mit<u>ch eat</u>s).

Easy: Write the following sentences and hints on the board. Work with students to find the hidden words *fish, gas, soil,* and *star*.

- Jeff is happy near the beach.
  (Hint: It swims and has scales.)
- Keep the water boiling as you cook.
  (Hint: It's a form of matter, like air.)
- I'm so ill that I can't help in the garden.
  (Hint: Plants grow in this.)
- She lost a ring on that dark night.
  (Hint: It's a bright object in the night sky.)

Average: Have students work in small groups to come up with sentences and hints for the words *fish, gas, soil,* and *star*.

Challenge: Have students work in pairs, looking through the word cards for 2–4 words to hide in sentences. They can then exchange papers with their partners to find one another's hidden words.

Decoding Activities

7. Sorting Center

Grouping: Individual or pairs

Materials: word cards, index cards, crayons or colored markers

Give students a set of word cards to sort. Explain that they need to listen to the sounds in the word on each card to sort them. Tailor the number of cards and the sorting task to their abilities, as described below.

Easy: On each of three index cards, have students draw and label a picture of an animal whose name ends with a target consonant sound, such as *deer, lion,* and *seal*. Then give students 6–8 cards with words that end with one of those 3 sounds. Have them sort the cards by ending sounds, placing each card under the appropriate animal.

Average: Give students 8–10 cards with one-syllable words. Ask them to sort the cards into groups that contain the same vowel sounds. You might model identifying two cards that contain matching vowel sounds, such as *speed* and *heat*.

Harcourt

Challenge: Give students a target syllable sound to look for, such as the əl in *animal* and *apple*. Have them pull out any word cards that contain words that end with this sound and then sort them by their spelling of əl. When they are done, they might try to think of other words that have the same spelling or other spellings of the əl sound.

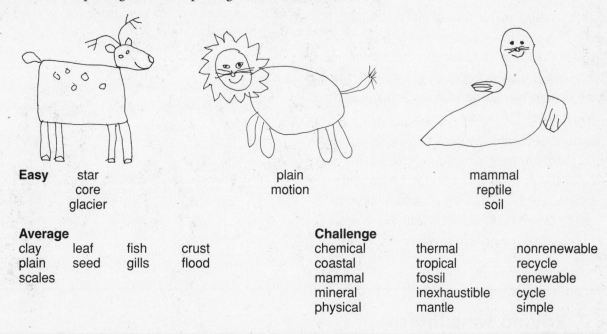

Easy
star
core
glacier

plain
motion

mammal
reptile
soil

Average

clay	leaf	fish	crust
plain	seed	gills	flood
scales			

Challenge

chemical	thermal	nonrenewable
coastal	tropical	recycle
mammal	fossil	renewable
mineral	inexhaustible	cycle
physical	mantle	simple

8. Syllable Sort

Grouping: Large or small group

Materials: word cards, access to a dictionary

Have students play a card game in which they collect words according to the number of syllables they hear. Have student partners deal 6–8 word cards and put the remaining words in a pile face down. Tell them to take turns choosing a card from the top of the deck, and deciding whether to keep or discard it. For example, a player collecting two-syllable words would discard a one- or three-syllable word. Discarded cards should be placed face up in a pile. The next player can choose from the word card deck or from the top of the discard pile.

The game ends when one player or the other has a complete set of words with the same number of syllables.

Easy: Limit the activity to 1- and 2-syllable words. Have pairs of students practice clapping out the number of syllables in some familiar words (book, ruler, pencil, chalk) before they begin sorting the word cards.

Average: Give students a chance to review the word cards before the game begins. If they are not sure how many syllables are in a word (such as *temperature*), they should consult a glossary or dictionary.

Challenge: Limit the activity to 3- and 4-syllable words. You may wish to provide time for students to review the vocabulary words before they begin the game.

9. Word Equations

Grouping: Whole class or large group (Easy), small group (Average and Challenge)

Materials: chalk; paper and pencil (Average and Challenge)

Students can use structural analysis to chunk multisyllabic words, creating "equations" that consist of the following:

prefix(es) + root word + suffix = word.

Write the equation on the board and review it with students. To the side, write *Prefixes* and list *con-*, *ex-/e-*, *in-*, *pro-*, and *re-*. Then

write *Suffixes* and list three entries: *-or/-er,*
-ation/-tion, -able/-ible. Use *condensation* to
model for students how to create an equation
(con + dens + ation = condensation).

Easy: Display these word cards: *revolution,*
insulator, conductor, renewable resource,
constellation, conservation, producer. Work on
the board with students to "analyze" the words
with both prefixes and suffixes. Help students
to write their equations.

Average: Have students work in small groups to
find words in their word cards that have at least
one of the prefixes listed on the board *and* one
of the suffixes listed. They should then work
together to write equations for these words.
Provide time for groups to share and compare
their work.

Challenge: Students should follow the procedure described in the Average option. They can
then work to come up with other words that
contain one of the prefixes listed and one of the
suffixes listed, writing equations for each word
they think of.

10. Rhyme Time Match

Grouping: Whole class or large group (Easy),
pairs (Average and Challenge)

Materials: word cards, chalk; 4 x 6 index cards
cut in half, pencils (Average and Challenge)

Have students work with different spellings for
the same phoneme as they match up rhyming
words. Display the following word cards: *bird,*
clay, core, flood, force, front, gas, loam, mass,
prey, scales, trait, weight.

Easy: Pick out the word *trait,* and help students
find a word that rhymes (weight). List these
two words on the board, noting the different
spellings for the phoneme āt. Follow a similar
procedure with *clay/prey* and *gas/mass.* For each
remaining word, have students suggest rhymes;
pick out and list a word that has a different
spelling for the phoneme (examples: bird/word,
core/roar, flood/mud, force/horse, front/hunt,
scales/tails).

Average: Along with the displayed word cards,
list these words on the board: *word, roar, mud,*
horse, hunt, home, tails. Have students work in
pairs, and have partners work together to write
each word on a separate index card. When they
are done, they should shuffle the "deck" and
place the cards face down in a 4 × 5 grid. They
can then play a matching game with rhyming
words: Player 1 turns over two random cards. If
the words rhyme, the player has made a match,
takes the cards, and goes again. If not, play goes
to the partner. When all the cards have been
matched, the player with the most pairs wins.

Challenge: Have student partners come up with
their own 10 rhyming pairs. Tell them that the
rhyming parts of the words have to be spelled
differently; use *trait/weight, prey/clay,* and
mass/gas as examples. Then have them write on
cards and play the matching game, as described
in the Average option.

Harcourt

Vocabulary Cards

root	simple plant
stem	seed
leaf	germinate
cell	seedling

[sim′pəl plant′]
A plant that has no roots, stems, or leaves (A14)

[ro͞ot]
The part of a plant that holds the plant in the ground and takes in water and minerals from the soil (A7)

[sēd]
The first stage in the growth of many plants (A18)

[stem]
A plant part that connects the roots with the leaves of a plant; it carries water from the roots to other parts of the plant (A7)

[jûr′mə·nāt′]
When a new plant breaks out of the seed (A21)

[lēf]
A plant part that grows out of the stem; it takes in the air and light that a plant needs (A7)

[sēd′ling]
A young plant (A21)

[sel]
The small unit that makes up all living things (A8)

Harcourt

photosynthesis	mammal
chlorophyll	bird
inherit	amphibian
trait	gills

[mam´əl] An animal that has fur or hair and is fed milk from its mother's body (A52)	[fōt´ō·sin´thə·sis] The food-making process of plants (A28)
[bûrd] An animal that has feathers, two legs, and wings (A55)	[klôr´ə·fil´] The substance that gives plants their green color; it helps a plant use energy from the sun to make food (A28)
[am·fib´ē·ən] An animal that begins life in the water and moves onto land as an adult (A60)	[in·her´it] To receive traits from parents (A48)
[gilz] A body part found in fish and young amphibians that takes in oxygen from the water (A61)	[trāt] A body feature that an animal inherits; it can also be some things that an animal does (A48)

Harcourt

fish	hibernate
scales	migrate
reptile	camouflage
instinct	mimicry

[hī′bər·nāt′] To enter a deep sleep in which life activities slow down (A69)	[fish] An animal that lives its whole life in water and breathes with gills (A62)
[mī′grāt′] To travel as a group from one place to live in another (A70)	[skālz] The small, thin, flat plates that help protect the bodies of fish and reptiles (A62)
[kam′ə·fläzh′] A natural disguise some animals have to help them blend in with their surroundings (A72)	[rep′tīl] A land animal that has dry skin covered by scales (A63)
[mim′ik·rē] The imitation by one animal of another animal or an object in order to avoid predators (A72)	[in′stingkt] A behavior an animal knows how to do without being taught (A68)

Harcourt

extinct	fossil
species	environment
endangered	ecosystem
threatened	population

[fos'əl]
Evidence of a plant or an animal that lived long ago on Earth (A77)

[ik·stingkt']
Describes a species that is gone forever because all of its kind have died (A76)

[in·vī'rən·mənt]
The things, both living and non-living, that surround a living thing (B6)

[spē'shēz]
A name that identifies a living organism (A76)

[ek'ō·sis'təm]
The living and nonliving things in an environment (B7)

[en·dān'jərd]
In danger of becoming extinct (A76)

[pop'yoo·lā'shən]
A group of the same kind of living things that all live in one place at the same time (B7)

[thret'ənd]
On the way to becoming endangered or extinct (A77)

Harcourt

community	tropical rain forest
habitat	coastal forest
forest	coniferous forest
deciduous forest	desert

[trop′i·kəl rān′fôr′ist]
A hot, wet forest where the trees grow very tall and their leaves stay green all year (B16)

[kə·myōō′nə·tē]
All the populations of organisms that live in an ecosystem (B7)

[kōs′təl fôr′ist]
A thick forest with tall trees that gets a lot of rain and does not get very warm or cold (B17)

[hab′ə·tat′]
The place where a population lives in an ecosystem (B7)

[kō·nif′ər·əs fôr′ist]
A forest in which most of the trees are conifers (cone-bearing) and stay green all year (B18)

[fôr′ist]
An area in which the main plants are trees (B14)

[dez′ərt]
An ecosystem where there is very little rain (B22)

[dē·sij′ōō·əs fôr′ist]
A forest in which most of the trees lose and regrow their leaves each year (B15)

grassland	producer
salt water	consumer
fresh water	herbivore
interact	carnivore

[prə·dōōs′ər] **A living thing that makes its own food (B51)**	[gras′land′] **An ecosystem made up of large, flat areas of land that are covered with grass (B28)**
[kən·sōōm′ər] **A living thing that eats other living things as food (B51)**	[sôlt′ wô′tər] **Water that has a lot of salt in it (B34)**
[hûr′bə·vôr′] **An animal that eats plants (B51)**	[fresh′ wôt′ər] **Water that has very little salt in it (B34)**
[kär′nə·vôr′] **An animal that eats other animals (B52)**	[in′tər·akt′] **When plants and animals affect one another or the environment to meet their needs (B50)**

Harcourt

omnivore	food web
decomposer	predator
food chain	prey
energy pyramid	mineral

Harcourt

[fōōd′ web′]
A model that shows how food chains overlap (B62)

[äm′ni·vôr′]
An animal that eats both plants and other animals (B52)

[pred′ə·tər]
An animal that hunts another animal for food (B62)

[dē′kəm·pōz′er]
A living thing that breaks down dead organisms for food (B52)

[prā]
An animal that is hunted by a predator (B62)

[fōōd′ chān′]
The path of food from one living thing to another (B56)

[min′ər·əl]
An object that is solid, is formed in nature, and has never been alive (C6)

[en′ər·jē pir′ə·mid]
A diagram that shows that the amount of useable energy in an ecosystem is less for each higher animal in the food chain (B58)

Harcourt

rock	igneous rock
crust	sedimentary rock
mantle	metamorphic rock
core	rock cycle

[ig′nē·əs rok′] **A rock that was once melted rock but has cooled and hardened (C12)**	[rok] **A solid made of minerals (C8)**
[sed′ə·men′tər·ē rok′] **A rock formed from material that has settled into layers and been squeezed until it hardens into rock (C12)**	[krust] **The solid outside layer of the Earth (C8)**
[met′ə·môr′fik rok′] **A rock that has been changed by heat and pressure (C12)**	[man′təl] **The middle layer of the Earth (C8)**
[rok′ sī′kəl] **The process in which one type of rock changes into another type of rock (C14)**	[kôr] **The center of the Earth (C8)**

Harcourt

fossil	**canyon**
mountain	**plain**
landform	**plateau**
valley	**barrier island**

[kan′yən]
A landform; a deep valley with very steep sides (C35)

[fos′əl]
Something that has lasted from a living thing that died long ago (C20)

[plān]
A landform; a flat area on Earth's surface (C35)

[moun′tən]
A landform; a place on Earth's surface that is much higher than the land around it (C35)

[pla·tō′]
A landform; a flat area higher than the land around it (C35)

[land′fôrm′]
A natural shape or feature of Earth's surface (C34)

[bar′ē·ər ī′lənd]
A landform; a thin island along a coast (C35)

[val′ē]
A landform; a lowland area between higher lands, such as mountains (C35)

Harcourt

weathering	volcano
erosion	flood
glacier	soil
earthquake	humus

Harcourt

[vol·kā′nō] **An opening in Earth's surface from which lava flows (C49)**	[we<u>th</u>′ər·ing] **The process by which rock is worn down and broken apart (C40)**
[flud] **A large amount of water that covers normally dry land (C50)**	[i·rō′zhən] **The movement of weathered rock and soil (C42)**
[soil] **The loose material in which plants can grow in the upper layer of Earth (C62)**	[glā′shər] **A huge sheet of ice (C44)**
[hyo͞o′məs] **The part of the soil made up of decayed parts of once-living things (C62)**	[ûrth′kwāk′] **The shaking of Earth's surface caused by movement of the crust and mantle (C48)**

Harcourt

topsoil	resource
bedrock	conservation
clay	strip cropping
loam	contour plowing

[rē′sôrs]
A material that is found in nature and that is used by living things (C88, C74)

[top′soil′]
The top layer of soil made up of the smallest grains and the most humus (C63)

[kon′ser·vā′shən]
The saving of resources by using them carefully (C76)

[bed′räk′]
The solid rock that is under soil (C63)

[strip′ krop′ing]
A type of planting that uses strips of thick grass or clover between strips of crops (C76)

[klā]
A type of soil made up of very small grains; it holds water well (C69)

[kon′tōor plou′ing]
A type of plowing for growing crops; creates rows of crops around the sides of a hill instead of up and down (C76)

[lōm]
A type of topsoil that is rich in minerals and has lots of humus (C70)

Harcourt

resource	recycle
renewable resource	groundwater
reusable resource	estuary
nonrenewable resource	evaporation

[rē·sī′kəl] **To reuse a resource to make something new (C100)**	[rē′sôrs] **A material that is found in nature and that is used by living things (C88, C74)**
[ground′ wôt′ər] **A form of fresh water that is found under Earth's surface (D8)**	[ri·nōō′ə·bəl rē′sôrs] **A resource that can be replaced in a human lifetime (C94)**
[es′chōō·er′·ē] **A place where fresh water from a river mixes with salt water from the ocean (D12)**	[rē·yōō′zə·bəl rē′sôrs] **A resource such as air or water that can be used over and over and can't be used up (C94)**
[ē·vap′ə·rā′shən] **The process by which a liquid changes into a gas (D17, E18)**	[non′ri·nōō′ə·bəl rē′sôrs] **A resource; such as coal or oil, that will be used up someday (C96)**

Harcourt

condensation	weather
precipitation	temperature
water cycle	front
atmosphere	wind

[we<u>th</u>ʹər] **The happenings in the atmosphere at a certain time (D32)**	[konʹdən·sāʹshən] **The changing of a gas into a liquid (D17)**
[temʹpər·ə·chər] **The measure of how hot or cold something is (D36)**	[prē·sipʹə·tāʹshən] **The water that falls to Earth as rain, snow, sleet, or hail (D18)**
[frunt] **A place where two air masses of different temperatures meet (D37)**	[wôtʹər sīʹkəl] **The movement of water from Earth's surface into the air and back to the surface again (D18)**
[wind] **The movement of air (D40)**	[atʹməs·firʹ] **The air that surrounds Earth (D30)**

anemometer	planet
weather map	asteroid
solar system	comet
orbit	rotation

[plan'it]
A large body of rock or gas that orbits the sun (D58)

[an'ə·mom'ə·tər]
An instrument that measures wind speed (D40)

[as'tər·oid]
A chunk of rock that orbits the sun (D64)

[weth'ər map']
A map that shows weather data for a large area (D46)

[kom'it]
A large ball of ice and dust that orbits the sun (D64)

[sō'lər sis'təm]
The sun, and the objects that orbit around it (D58)

[rō·tā'shən]
The spinning of an object on its axis (D68)

[ôr'bit]
The path an object takes as it moves around another object in space (D58)

Harcourt

axis	solar eclipse
revolution	matter
phases	physical property
lunar eclipse	solid

[sō′lər i·klips′]
The hiding of the sun that occurs when the moon passes between the sun and Earth (D80)

[ak′sis]
An imaginary line that goes through the North Pole and the South Pole of Earth (D68)

[mat′ər]
Anything that takes up space (E6)

[rev′ə·lōō′shən]
The movement of one object around another object (D68)

[fiz′i·kəl prop′ər·tē]
Anything you can observe about an object by using your senses (E6)

[fāz·əz]
The different shapes the moon seems to have in the sky when observed from Earth (D76)

[sol′id]
A form of matter that takes up a specific amount of space and has a definite shape (E11)

[lōō′nər i·klips′]
The hiding of the moon when it passes through the Earth's shadow (D78)

Harcourt

liquid	volume
gas	mass
atom	physical change
evaporation	mixture

[vol′yo͞om] **The amount of space that matter takes up (E22)**	[lik′wid] **A form of matter that has volume that stays the same, but can change its shape (E12)**
[mas] **The amount of matter in an object (E24)**	[gas] **A form of matter that does not have a definite shape or a definite volume (E12)**
[fiz′i·kəl chānj] **A change to matter in which no new kinds of matter are formed (E40)**	[at′əm] **The basic building block of matter (E16)**
[miks′chər] **A substance that contains two or more different types of matter (E41)**	[ē·vap′ə·rā′shən] **The process by which a liquid changes into a gas (D17, E18)**

Harcourt

solution	kinetic energy
chemical change	electricity
energy	fossil fuel
potential energy	vibrate

[ki·net′ik en′ər·jē]
The energy of motion (F6)

[sə·lōō′shən]
**A mixture in which the particles
of two different kinds of matter
mix together evenly (E42)**

[i·lek′tris′i·tē]
**A form of energy that people
produce from the active energy
of wind and moving water and
the stored energy in oil and coal
(F7)**

[kem′i·kəl chānj′]
**A change that forms different
kinds of matter (E46)**

[fos′əl fyōō′əl]
**Fuel formed from the remains
of once-living organisms (F8)**

[en′ər·jē]
The ability to cause change (F6)

[vī′brāt′]
**To move quickly back and forth,
producing sound (F19)**

[pō·ten′shəl en′ər·jē]
**The energy an object has because
of its position or its shape (F6)**

circuit	friction
waste heat	conduction
thermal energy	conductor
heat	insulator

Harcourt

[frik′shən] **The force between two moving objects that makes it hard for the objects to move (F41)**	[sûr′kit] **The path electricity follows from a battery through a bulb and back to the battery (F20)**
[kən·duk′shən] **The movement of thermal energy from one object to another where they touch (F46)**	[wāst′hēt′] **The heat produced when a machine works to convert fuel energy into the energy of motion (F26)**
[kən·duk′tər] **A material in which thermal energy moves easily (F47)**	[thûr′məl en′ər·jē] **The energy that moves the particles in matter (F39)**
[in′sə·lāt′ər] **A material in which thermal energy does not move easily (F47)**	[hēt] **The movement of thermal energy from one place to another (F40)**

Harcourt

convection	motion
radiation	speed
thermometer	gravity
force	weight

[mō′shən]
A change in position (F67)

[kən·vek′shən]
The movement of thermal energy from one place to another in moving liquids and gases (F48)

[spēd]
The measure of how fast something moves over a certain distance (F69)

[rā′dē·ā′shən]
The movement of thermal energy without any objects touching or moving (F48)

[grav′i·tē]
The force that pulls objects toward each other (F70)

[thûr·mom′ə·tər]
A tool used to measure temperature (F52)

[wāt]
The measure of the pull of gravity on an object (F70)

[fôrs]
A push or a pull (F66)

Harcourt

work	
simple machine	
lever	
inclined plane	

	[wûrk] **The measure of force that it takes to move an object a certain distance (F74)**
	[sim′pəl mə·shēn′] **A tool that helps people do work (F78)**
	[lev′ər] **A bar that moves on or around a fixed point (F78)**
	[in·klīnd′ plān′] **A simple machine made of a flat surface set at an angle to another surface (F79)**

PHYSICAL PROPERTIES CHARTS FOR WB 220

	It Looks				It Feels			
Object	Shiny	Dull	Color		Hard	Soft	Rough	Smooth
penny								
marble								
book								
index card								
key								
pepper								
nickel								
uncooked macaroni								
candy								
cotton								
twist tie								

	It Smells				It Sounds			
Object	Sweet	Sharp	No smell		Loud	Soft	Makes a ping	No sound
penny								
marble								
book								
index card								
key								
pepper								
nickel								
uncooked macaroni								
candy								
cotton								
twist tie								

Harcourt

Flowchart

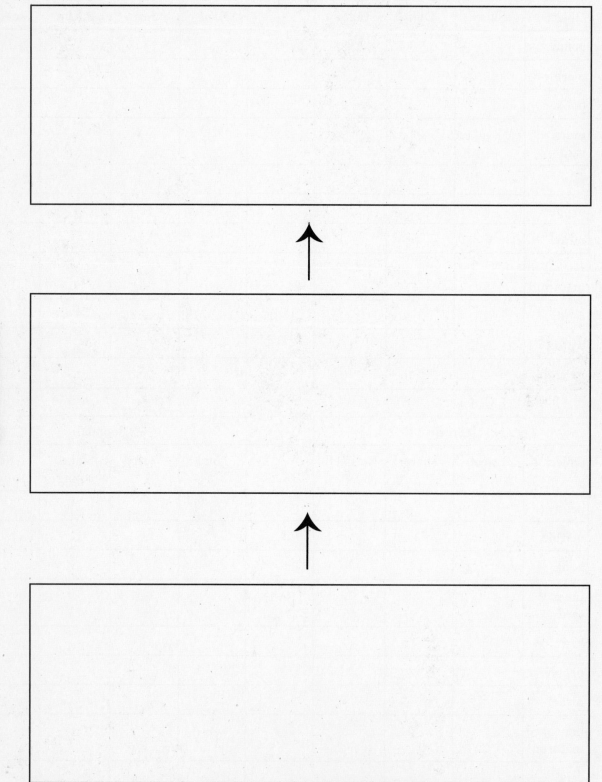

Venn Diagram

Computer Notes

K-W-L Chart

What I Know	What I Want to Know	What I Learned

Harcourt

Web

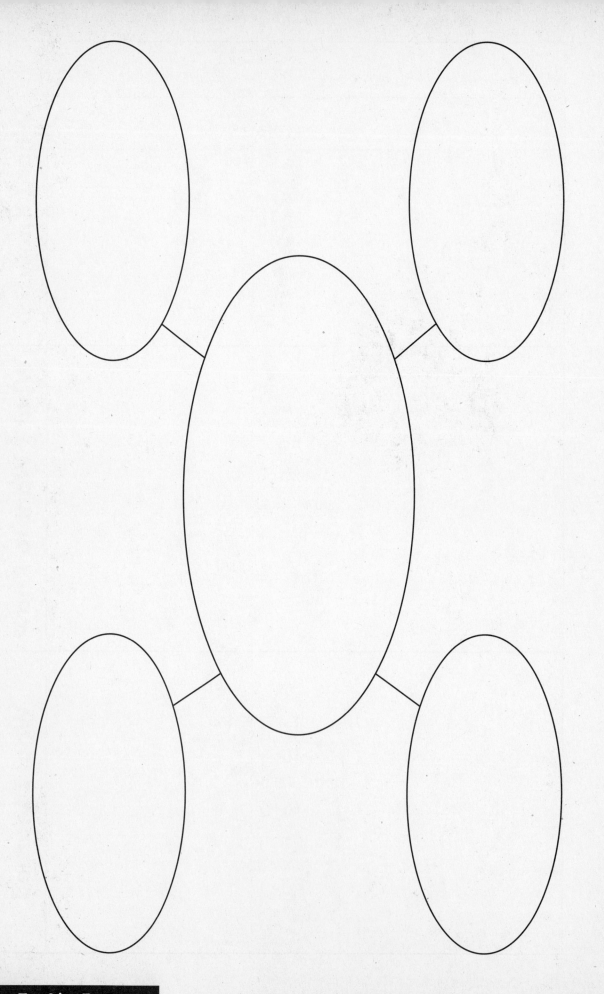

Chart

Knowledge Chart

Prior Knowledge About____	New Knowledge About____
1.	1.
2.	2.
3.	3.
4.	4.
5.	5.
6.	6.
7.	7.

Prediction Chart

What I Predict Will Happen	What Actually Happened

Project Plan

What We Want to Find Out

1.

How We Can Find Out

2.

What We Need to Do

3.	Materials

How We Can Share Information

4.

Harcourt

1-cm grid

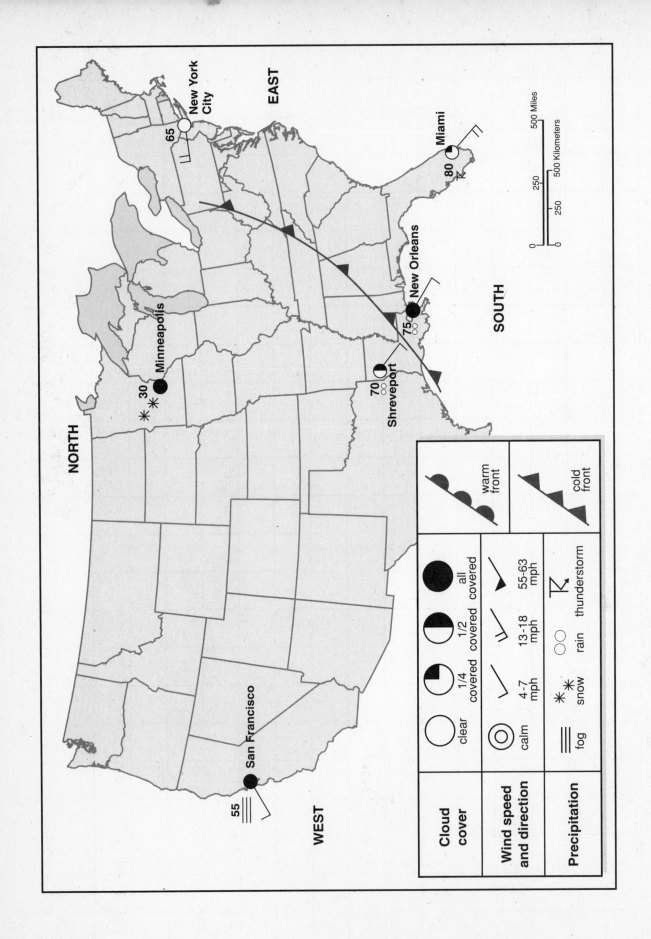

Use with pages D42–D43.